EL SHADDAI

MY ONE TRUE LOVE

BY

VICTORIA AMIDOU

El Shaddai
My One True Love
by
Victoria Amidou
P.O. Box 085137
Racine, Wisconsin 53408
www.victoriaamidou.com

This book or parts thereof may not be reproduced in any form, stored in a retrieval system or transmitted in any form by any means-electronic, mechanical, photocopy, recording or otherwise-without written permission of the publisher, except as provided by United States of America copyright law

Unless otherwise noted, all Scripture quotations are from the King James Version of the Bible. Copyright © 1979, by Thomas Nelson, Inc., publishers. Used by permission.

Copyright © 2016 by Victoria Amidou
Published February 14, 2016
Published in the Unites States of America 2016

ISBN-13: 978-0692636824

ISBN-10: 069263682X

CONTENTS

Acknowledgements
Introduction
1. Breaking The Cycle of Abuse - 1
2. Expecting The Unexpected - 10
3. Seasons - 19
4. Learning to Live Again - 28
5. Distance - 43
6. Contradictions - 51
7. Is It Really? - 58
8. People Pleaser - 65
9. To Thine Own Self Be True - 71
10. Reflection - 77
11. Wanting - 84
12. Honoring The Power of Two - 90
13. Expectation is Manifestation - 98
14. Christ not Karma - 105
15. Selfless - 110
16. Spirit Verses the Natural - 114
17. The Power of Suggestion - 120
18. A Virtuous Woman - 127
19. Attracting a True Man of God - 139
20. Who Holds the Key - 150
21. Hurry Up and Wait - 159
22. Acknowledge - 161
23. Decisions - 165
24. Preparations - 170
25. Moving Forward with God's Covering - 199
26. Backwards - 205
27. Knowing the Female Body - 219
28. Africa the Mother Land - 234
29. At Your Own Pace - 240
30. The Spiritual Importance of Sex - 244
    Appendix – Thankful - 259
    Notes - 261

« ACKNOWLEDGEMENTS »

I dedicate this book to El Shaddai. For without God I am nothing. It is through my relationship with my Creator that all things are possible. There is no greater love than that of my Source.

« INTRODUCTION »

I FINALLY GET IT! After battling with myself on this quest to find what I thought would be my one true love. A topic God so graciously gave me to write about. I foolishly thought that God meant a love between a man and his wife. Oh my God! After suffering such great defeat, betrayal, and abuse. I realized that my one true love is God! He is and has always been my El Shaddai. My love, my everything. The reason I exist, breath, touch, teach, cry, grieve, even bleed. Thank you, God, for showing me that you have always loved me, and now I can truly say that I love you with every fiber of my being. I totally surrender to You everything that I was, am, and hope to be. Thank You Lord. I finally get it! I am now okay with my less than perfect body, mind, life, existence. It is okay that I have failed more times than I have letters in my name. Life for me has not been easy. However, I have found a way to cope by praying to God. No, prayer is not a magic bullet that will make all of your troubles disappear, but it is the greatest step that you can take towards healing.

« 1 » BREAKING THE CYCLE OF ABUSE

There came a time in my life when I was so scared and overwhelmed that I didn't know how I was going to make it. There was nothing that anyone could have said or done that would have brought me out. I cried all the time. I was a functioning mess. Getting up to take care of my children and praying for night time to come so that I could lay down with my misery.

Fear controlled me and pain paralyzed me. I thought I was my worst enemy until I ran into another wolf in sheep clothing. I even now ask myself why did I allow this to happen to me when I very well knew that this was not the person for me. There was nothing about this person that I liked nor wanted. I was again settling. Creating more disaster in my life and another reason to fail. I was stuck in that self-destructive mode. Most would not admit to purposely destroying their lives. Causing the type of pain that leaves you gasping for air.

You can read this and say to yourself I would never

do that, oh no not me, she must be crazy. Well, guess what ladies, I am many of you, yes you. Stop lying to yourselves about your situation. Pretending like life is great and that you have it all together while inside everything is falling apart. I am about to say things that most wouldn't with the faith that someone out there will read this and healing will come from their pain.

I am not going to get into a big debate about what's right or what's wrong when it comes to my faith and my personal relationship with my God. I am indeed His vessel merely here for His glory. Now with that out of the way. Hmmm, let's get started.

I have learned that life is what you create. I created this mess as an adult by thinking negatively from listening to others constantly telling me what I was seeking was not realistic. Mind you these were the people who were supposed to be on my side and love me. I now overstand that they only told me what they knew. They too were settling, so my wanting better also forced them to look at their lives and see that it was not what they wanted either.

The difference between them and me was the fact that I was dreaming of coming out. I had a desire for better. I knew that God did not want this for me. It did not line up with the dreams that he had shown me. It's sad when you have no one that overstands the true pattern of abuse. They rationalized why and how the abuser treats them. They are afraid of being alone. To them, it is a strike against their womanhood. I have so much as heard this phrase most of my life, **"a**

no good man is better than no man any day." Wow, really? I must have thought this because every relationship I had was of no value. In some way, I was being abused.

Most abused women don't know their worth. In their mind, they have no value unless there is a man in their lives. There is this badge of honor that they wear when they have a man. For some, this is the only way that they feel of value, even if it is fake. They push aside the fact that this man is abusing them. They even go so far as to categorize different types of abuse to stay in the situation. I have been guilty of that behavior as well.

The truth of the matter is abuse is just that abuse. Whether it's calling you demeaning things or slapping you. No woman on this earth deserves to be hurt. You can make it on your own. You do deserve the kind of love that the Creator wants you to have.

There should never be a compromise when it comes to respect. Love builds, strengthens, encourages, shares, and cares. Love does not tear down, destroy, demean, belittle, kick, hit, nor control you in a negative manner. Love adds too; it does not take away from who you are.

I have come to a point in my life where I have begun the very painful process of retraining my mind to accept the goodness that God so graciously gives and says that I am to get from others. I know that I deserve better than what I have been getting and that I have a right to put out of my life anyone who mistreats me. They do not have to like my choice, but they will respect it.

Abusers use fear to control their victims, and it is debilitating. Fear makes you do strange things, I know first-hand. It will make you go back to the abuser when you know it is not the right thing to do. They are master manipulators. Experts at their craft. Insecure men using abuse as a power tool. Liars that will do anything to break down your self-esteem. It is the only way that the feel worthy. Breaking you down somehow gives them validation. They have low esteem, and they want to make sure that yours is lower than theirs. Mentally this makes them feel superior.

I have heard so many women say that love hurts, and that is one of the biggest lies ever told. We as a whole have to stop lying to ourselves. Abuse is never your fault, however, staying in it is. Fear keeps us in it, but faith brings us out. However, **"faith without works is dead."** We must pray and then we must do. Yes, doing what is required to get out of these situations is not easy. It is going to take courage and help from someone who is positive and compassionate.

Someone who can encourage you through those moments of doubt and not judge you for the way that you are feeling. If you have no one that you can confide in, then know without a shadow of a doubt that you can talk to God. He will hear you, and when you listen, you will hear him.

Breaking the cycle of abuse requires a great deal of

work. It requires you to dig deep within yourself to find that place where you first became broken. That place where you lost the true you. Abusers can sense this, and they study you to find your weakness. They are predators stalking their prey, and soon they will go in for the kill. They enter your life then they build you up from the information that they gained while studying you. It's just a part of their plot so, please don't believe the hype because the crash is coming.

It's like fattening the hog before the slaughter. Soon everything that they said to build you up becomes the very things that they use to tear you down. I heard a guy say before; **"first you build them, then you break them, and then you will have total control over them."**

Avoid such people. I know them very well because they are leeches. They are the ones that will suck the very life out of you.

The truth of the matter is that words do have the power to hurt. Words can cut you deeper than any knife. They go down to the very essence of who you are, to your soul. Abusers know this, and that is why they use this long before they use their fists. Their mouths are like poisonous snake venom. Spitting and spurring out negative words with lethal force. Words can harm you and can also help you. Abusers count on you not using your words. Keeping silent about the abuse gives them, even more, power.

No one knows, no one can help. Many women do not talk about their abuse because they are ashamed. So they suffer in silence and fear. Afraid to say or do anything that may cause the abuser to snap. The truth of the matter is, it doesn't matter what you do or don't do, an abuser is just that. Never underestimate your abuser. Don't allow fear to paralyze you. Use that fear, to strengthen your spirit. Start at this very moment developing a plan to leave this abusive relationship because it will not get better.

I know that there are moments in the relationship when he doesn't hit, belittle, and demean you. I also know that those moments are few and far between, and typically come when he senses that you are thinking of leaving. Abusers need you. Yes, they need you to feel powerful. Abusing you gives them a sense of false rulership. So they will do whatever is required to keep this power, and I don't mean this in a good way. Be very careful during this time of planning. They are watching you.

Try to use a phone where the phone numbers that you call he will not have access too. If you have friends and family you are still in contact with, start to back off shortly before your actual day to leave. Do not tell those that you love about your plan because you never know who he has as an ally. Also, you do not want those you love to be in danger. The mind of an abuser is a not rational. They think that you have in some way caused them to act this way. Which we know is not the truth.

You must know that if there is a threat to harm you, it is very likely that the abuser will carry it out. I can't stress this enough, only inform your loved ones about the leave after you have done so. Do not tell them where you are and block the number out that you are calling from so no one can call you back. No trail to your whereabouts should be left behind. Only bring what is necessary for your survival.

It is normal to feel whatever you are feeling. Just don't go back! You can and will make it with him. Keep thinking positive, even when everything around you doesn't appear that way. You have to be willing to do what is required to come out of this. Listen to that voice within that tells you when something is not right. Your spirit knows how to protect you, but you have to be willing to listen.

If you have children, do not tell them your plans. You do not want to take the chance that your children will tell. It is imperative that you remain as calm as possible and secretive. Planning is key to your survival.

The first things that you should get together are important papers. Birth certificates, social security cards, identification, cash, deeds, titles, medication, etc. Make sure that these items are readily available to you when the moment comes to leave. Never use you credit cards, bank cards, cell-phone.

These items can be used to track you. Be sure to get a prepaid phone for emergency purposes and do not give the number to your loved ones. Your family homes will be the first place that the abuser will look for you. Your friends will be next, and then coworkers. If you are employed, I suggest you take a leave of absence or transfer with strict orders that no one is to know your whereabouts. Make a checklist and write it in the code format where only you can overstand it just in case someone finds it. I know that this sounds like, a lot but trust me once you start to prepare it will all come together.

When you become discouraged, be sure to focus on the big picture. Your life and the lives of your children. Being free of the pain of abuse is a milestone. The first steps to healing are making up your mind to leave, and then following through with it. Trust yourself. I know that you can do this because I did it.

When abuse happens, your level of confidence decreases. You wonder how did you get to this point in your life. You feel ashamed, and often you think of dying. Suicidal thoughts run rampant. You wonder if you can make it out of this alive. If, is a very powerful two letter word. So powerful in fact that it can keep you stuck in an abusive relationship.

Let's discuss the if factor. If means in the event of or in the case of something. If also means that it is not absolute, there is a chance. If is the compass to everything that we are trying to accomplish. Be careful of people who use if in your situation. It is not a matter of if it is going to happen with God; it is a matter of when. When you are going through something, do not allow people to cast doubt on your knowledge of God by bringing in the negative factor of if, God is not looking for your if, He is looking for your when. Speak when into your situation that means that you are standing in faith that God will move on your behalf. It is a not a matter of if, it is a matter of when. Being a child of God, you must operate in faith. **"For without faith, it is impossible to please God."**

Man looks at the outer experience that's why we must ask God to create in us a clean heart so that we may have a renewing of our minds. The if of man must be connected to the willingness of man.

"The prayers of the righteous availeth much."

You must know that you are coming out of this. Know that this is a test and you will not be in this situation always. Rely on the Lord for He is your strength. Lean not unto your understanding and stop blaming yourself for being in the abuse. We all make mistakes. Trust God and keep praying. **"No weapon formed against you shall prosper."** It is only a matter of time before your abuser gets what's coming to him.

God assures that. I trust in miracles, and I know that dreams come true. I know with everything in me that God loves us. He will never leave us or forsake us. Just hold on and listen to your heart and not your head. The heart is where God resides. God will never lead you astray. Change starts the moment you decide to pray. We are speaking those things into existence. Prayer brings about the assurance that we trust in God. That we trust Him to do what He said He would do. Pray daily. Always begin your prayers by thanking and blessing God.

« 2 » EXPECTING THE UNEXPECTED

WHAT TO DO WHEN mistreated is inflicted upon you. There are times in our lives when the ones closest to us are our enemies. What happens when your whole family is trying to set you up? Trying to stop you from reaching your destiny? When you are trying to better yourself and live for the Lord, there are those who will try to kill your spirit when you do not comply with what they want. They are like lobsters in a tank. A lobster will start climbing to the top and the others in the tank will try to pull the one headed to the top back down. Some people are the same way.

They have no goals, drive, nor determination to excel. Nor do they want you to have any of those. They will spend time hindering you instead of working on bettering themselves. There is a chance that the people around you are spiritually illegal. Simply put, they are not sanctioned by God. The painful part of this knowledge is that these people may include your parents. There are some parents who see the gift in their children as an opportunity for financial gain. They pimp your gift. The money becomes the means for them to better themselves. Yes, your parents are entitled to some of your assets, but most of your earned income should be in an account for future use.

There are no limits when it comes to your dreams. Everything starts with a thought. Whatever you desire and it lines up with the will of God, you will have. There is nothing that anyone can do or say that can stop the will of God in your life. There may be obstacles along the way. Just know that as those obstacles come, that they are not denials. Everything is a part of God's plan for your life. Yes, even what looks like mistakes are all a part of God's plan for your life.

The Kingdom of God has three points, the outer courts, the inner courts, and the Holy of Holy. You must enter into the gates of the Lord with thanksgiving. Don't be ashamed to ask for what you need when in the presence of the Lord. You must be willing to put aside your shame and fear when going to God for anything. There is nothing too big or too small for God. Know that as a child of The Most High you can go to Him anytime.

Unfortunately, when we are hurting, feeling unworthy, shamed, etc., we sometimes tend to turn away from God. This is not the time to do so. When feeling this way, it is imperative that we pray, worship, and praise Him more than ever. The enemy attacks become even more aggressive when we are already at our lowest point. Satan does not fight fair.

The sooner this is realized, the more alert you will become. Remember that the enemy is not flesh and blood.

We wrestle against principalities and rulers of the darkness. Although when someone hurts us, we see them and not the demonic spirit that dwells within them. It can become very hard to separate the person from the deed that they have done. Forgiveness is the goal in which we are to obtain when faced with the anger of abuse and betrayal. Being able to forgive an individual who has turned your life upside down does not in no way mean that you have to let them back into your life.

It means that you have made a conscious choice to let go of the hurt and move on with your life. When you do this the person who maimed you no longer has any power over you. You will have to find a way to allow yourself to feel happiness again. It is okay to laugh again. Give yourself permission to be graceful, elegant, and loving.

Now you are free to move forward and heal the wounds that have plagued you. Letting go and letting God shows you just how blessed you are, it's a wonderful feeling. Allow Him to show you how to love yourself unconditionally again. Break down all the barriers that you have. Start by accepting your faults, flaws, and mistakes. These errors have made you who you are today.

You are stronger and wiser. Ready to step into God's destiny for you. You have gone through these trials so that you can help someone else come out. As sad as it sounds, there is, unfortunately, another woman who is or is about to become the old you. God! Have mercies on their souls.

Expectations of the bad will leave you filled with anxiety. When you have accepted abuse repeatedly, the pain of it is all that you know. So you tend to gravitate subconsciously towards it. Choosing men that will inflict more pain on you. I know it sounds outlandish, but it is the truth. We abused women often ask, "why do I always end up with abusive men?" We also ask, "why do I always attract the abusive men?"

When there is abuse, you have this internal magnet that draws upon that which it knows. Abusers can sense this in you, and they prey upon it. You will continue to attract these types of men until you heal from the abuse. Once you make the choice to start the healing process you must dig deep within yourself and ask this very painful question "is the person I am with, abusive towards me?" If the answer to that question is yes, then you must decide what is your next step to healing.

How can you effectively start your healing process with an abuser still in your life? You are trying to rid your mind, body, and soul of this abusive circle. You need the space to do that, and you can't do that when you are still in an abusive relationship. Breaking this cycle is not easy, but you can do it, you must be willing to do the unexpected. Leave! It is not easy to leave everything that you know, but it is vital to your healing process.

You will feel a vast array of emotions; that will range from sadness to rage. These emotions are normal and healthy. Acknowledging these emotions and allowing them to come out is a must to your healing process.

Only you know how you feel, and only you can make the choice to change what you are feeling. Give power to your pain by acknowledging it and then use it to empower yourself. Take back your life by aggressively pursuing your healing. Don't allow anyone to stop you from doing what is vital to your survival. Ask God to be your strength and guidance. Know that all things are possible when you trust God. Eliminate that if factor and hold onto the when factor. You will come out of this.

There is something to be said about a man who uses scare tactics to keep a woman with him. Just as an abuser uses fear, a good man uses love. A man who loves you will nurture and protect you, so much so that you will not want to be with anyone else. Love changes the way an abused woman sees herself. Her confidence builds. She no longer holds onto the fear that was used to paralyzed her.

Love is very powerful and in any relationship it is to be given as well as received. I have heard many people say that love is not enough to hold a relationship together. I disagree. Based on what the Holy Bible says; God is love! So with God being love then God can surely hold your relationship together. However, God has to be in the relationship. When

God in the center of your life, everything in your life operates around Him.

God is the foundation for which all things positive are built. When placing God in your life, you are operating on the fact that faith will sustain you. Praying, praising, worshiping, and studying the word are paramount in your relationship with God.

Putting God first places you in a position to better see your obstacles and challenges through fresh eyes. It requires a great deal of motivation to allow the Holy Spirit to lead you. Especially when there is so much negativity going on. Whether it be television, radio, workplace, friends, family, etc. You have to stay focused.

There are times when it will appear that your spirituality is working against you. This is not the truth. There are dark evil forces working to keep you from reaching your greatest potential. When those moments of doubt come and they will, you must pray more and press forward. Stay focused on the promises of God. Use positive affirmations to motivate you. **"Yes, we can"** was the phrase used in the 2008 Obama campaign and it changed this nation.

Words are very powerful. Words can crush a person's spirit, and words can change a nation. Be careful which words you choose to use. Speak life and not death. Go hard on the positivity, it won't hurt, try it. "'I can be whatever I want to be." "I can do whatever I want to do." "I can have whatever I want to have." That's it, keep going. You can do it. Self-motivation is the best motivation. Take these three steps and see what happens. You have nothing too loose.

"Write the vision and make it plain." Do just that. Make a detailed list of the things that you want to do with your life. Keep your list with you at all times and read it out loud to yourself. This is a declaration. You are declaring to the Universe that this is your decree. Okay, now you have achieved two of the three steps to change. Now do it!

Find a way to make your dreams come true. Do research on whatever it is that you want. Find pictures of that dream and look at them constantly. If it is a place that you want to go, then get on the internet and go to Google Earth. I am amazed every time that I visit this site because I can go anywhere in the world without leaving the comfort of my home. There are moments when I do this that I become so overwhelmed by the awesomeness of God. The knowledge that He has given humans is powerful.

I can stroll down the streets of Paris, fly to Costa Rica, cruise the Atlanta Ocean, climb the highest Mountain. You get the picture. Also, read more, get books that are the topic of your goals. Nothing fails but a try. Remember that just because you fail at something once or twice doesn't necessarily mean that you will fail if you try again. Never give up on your dreams, it doesn't matter how far away you may seem to be away from them. Love yourself enough to fight for whatever dreams that you have. Know that having perseverance makes all things are possible. When we become older when sometimes think that it is foolish to daydream about what could be. I think this could not be further from the truth. It is because of this that one may struggle with pursuing their dreams. It is healthy to have an imagination and to dream of what could be.

Negativity is not a part of this equation. Do not allow your age, marital status, financial situation, ethnicity, or origin, stop you from knowing that you can have what you want. There are no limits when you know that you can. I pray that you do not allow your past to stop you from believing in yourself. As abused women, we sometimes think back on the abuser's words and began to doubt our ability to do that which we were chosen to do. When these times arise, you must redirect your mind by remembering that you are a child of God and the Chains no longer bind you that Satan used to hold you captive.

Your freedom is yours, and no one has the right to hinder you from moving forward. Know that everything is a lesson that you can either use to hinder you or propel you into your destiny. Some of the most beautiful things on this earth friction played at part in developing. There is sometimes pain involved in the process of evolving. However, this pain and friction are not meant to be permanent. Everything has a season, and when you keep this in mind, it will help you stay focused.

The Bible is considered the book of life. It is an instruction manual telling us what we need to do in every situation in life. It is there to be of guidance to us and warns us of what is to come. The Creator has instilled in us the gift of the Holy Spirit. The Holy Spirit is the voice inside that warns us of danger and guides us towards blessings. When you grow, you are to become more in tune with the Holy Spirit. Some would call this your intuition. Listen to your body because we all have that internal alarm that lets us know when we need to rest, flee, laugh, and even cry.

« 3 » SEASONS

LOOK AT YOUR LIFE and the events in it as the four seasons. Winter is the first season of the year, spring is the second, summer is the third, and fall is the fourth. Winter is a time of death. In nature, nothing grows. It is a time of resting. When the days are shorter and the nights are longer. Often referred to as the season of depression. Winter our darkest before dawn place. The place in our lives where we have to hold on tightly to our faith. The place where the abuse, betrayal, defeat, doubt happened. No, not literally but figuratively.

This is space in time where our lives are frozen and at a stand-still. Where we are thinking of what needs to be done and changed. Wondering when our dreams will manifest themselves. This season is a season of thought and often these thoughts will lead to regret and also dread. Regretting the failures and disappointments, dreading the work that is required to change the things that can be. You must hold on because change is coming. Use this time to rest for the next season will require plenty of physical work.

This season is the season of less. When in the power of less it is imperative that you do not consume more than you have stored up. You are not producing at this time and therefore, in this winter season in your life you will benefit the least. You are going to have to put limits on yourself. Especially on your time. Limit the time you use on non-essential things. You must even limit your limits. Re-challenge your mind to make you significant.

Spring is our second season of the year. A time for birth, renewing, more light than dark. A place of coming out. A place where you can see things clearer. A season of awakening. A season of shedding that which was old and bringing forth that which is new. A time to stop and smile the flowers because they are in bloom. Dressing lighter and feeling free of the bulkiness and all the extra baggage. It's amazing how a woman's body is in tune with the forces of nature. We are truly a unique being. God entrusted us with the gift of birth. We have the ability to bring forth life. Springtime is a time of sowing, planting, planning, preparing for what is to come. The anticipation of what will be.

Everything about spring is about timing. It is a time of flourishing. You must do everything in preparation for what is to come which is ultimately reaping, which we will discuss in greater detail in our last season. However, doing more things does not make you successful. Do not confuse activity with achievement.

You will have to figure out what you are going to do. Either a whole lot incomplete things or focus all of your energy on one thing.

I have learned from Japanese poetry that **5, 7, 5 are 17 syllables with three lines about nature called Haiku [traditional]. It teaches you about limits, to give what is needed by minimizing what you say in three lines. You give what is required. It has broken this down into three simple principles. 1: by setting limits you are going to choose what's necessary. 2: what am I doing, that will produce an impact and can I make an impact with minimal resources. 3: strategically working the less to create more and making it work for me.**

Season three is upon us now. It is summer. Things are in full blown, the birds are soaring, the sun is scorching, and there is plenty of activity in your life. The list of things to do is boundless. The warm weather makes you happy. The sun has kissed your face, and you feel unstoppable. Summer is a time of playfulness in your life. You have shed that old skin, and you are radiant again. You have many dreams and goals to accomplish. You are looking forward to living again and all of it possibilities, but wait you have to keep in mind that you must have limits. When thinking of limits, most would assume that it is the limited of something that is bad. However, in life limits must be placed on the good as well.

In setting limits, you will simplify your life. Start with your closet. Go to your closet and look inside. If your closet is a mess, then so is your life. Start simplifying your life today by setting limits in your closet. Take the time to reflect upon what is needed, then get rid of what is not. Take what you no longer need to the local homeless shelter or Goodwill store. By donating, you become a blessing to someone else. Didn't that feel good? Now with that out of the way let's move on.

In dealing with your limitations, you must put your focus on you. When you are stressed, take a moment to reflex on what you are feeling. Now ask yourself am I stressed because I did not limit myself in any area of my life? The answer is going to be yes. Overextending yourself will cause stress. Do only what you can with limitations for that day. Pace yourself in all areas of your life.

You must always place a value on your time. Time is your most precious resource. Spend it wisely because once it is gone, you can't get it back. If a person does not value your time, they do not value you. You must overstand that your time is valuable.

Also, if a person claims to love you and make their choice not to spend time with you, they have just placed you in their least of valuable, category. You are an option to them, not a priority. Those that do not make you a priority in their lives no matter who they are do not need to be a priority in your life. You must eliminate those who take up valuable time in your life when they are not affording you the same luxury. Do not be afraid to place the people in your life. No one has the right to take from you that which is precious, your time.

Autumn or fall as some would refer to it as a time of harvest. The season in which you will reap what you have sowed literally. Farmers anticipate this because it is very vital to their livelihood. All that they have planted in the spring time has now grown to maturity and is ready to harvest. What they have done to prepare for this season has required a great deal of hard work and planning. Well, so have we. We have to wait for this moment.

Harvest time in the spiritual is when all that we have been praying for has now manifested itself into the physical. All of the tears, studying, planning, and praying has brought us to this moment. Autumn is also a time for reflection as well as all the other seasons. It's just that with each season the reflection if different. It's like dressing every day and looking at your reflection in the mirror. It's you but with a new outfit, which has brought about a new outlook.

Autumn is also a time of shedding, like death, as you will. In preparation for the winter. The long days of summer have gone. The time has shifted back. The days have become shorter. The temperature has begun to fall. No more summer wear, swimsuits, nor walks by the lake without a light jacket, or sweater. Unlike the farmer, we may stay in one season far longer than they do. It may take us years to come out. We may have to encounter some serious obstacles. Sometimes the farmer faces challenges and obstacles as well. Whether it be drought, bad seeds, flooding, infestations, etc.

Being stuck into between seasons too long can be

very disheartening. During these times, you must exercise your faith by not focusing on what you see but rather focusing on what you don't see. Think of the dreams, goals, and future. You have to remember that there are some things in your life that you can't control. There are two forces in your life. One is working for you [God] and one working against you [Satan].

There will always be both positive and negative forces in your life. However, keeping this in mind will help you to overstand yourself and the course of events in your life.

Learning your lesson, the first time when it comes to mistakes is paramount. Your limits will make you more effective. You will not be able to set limits for your life until you know your value. Always keep in mind that anyone that values you will also value your time. Whatever you are in, make sure that it is giving back what you put into it.

Everything in life should yield a return. When dating the goal should be a marriage. When going to college, the goal should be a degree. When purchasing property, the goal should be ownership. You get the picture. Seed time and harvest. Ask yourself what is important to you? What is the one thing that, can't be touched? Setting boundaries allows you to receive what is best for you. If you do not want a man with children already, then do not go out on dates with men that have them.

Stick to your decision, no matter what. These limits

will allow you to eliminate the have nots before they can take root in your life. Only you know what you can and can't handle. Know your worth. Know the difference between your needs and your wants. You can aim high, just make sure that you are realistic. Always do an inventory of your life. Ask yourself what should you eliminate from your life? Then ask yourself who needs to eliminated? Then delete unnecessary people. Those that are not with you are against you. Do not maintain relationships with people who do not respect who you are as a person. Those that can't be there for you when you are going through do not need to be present when you come out.

The greatest enemy during your seasons is the middle. Now is your year to come out. You will fight your greatest fight. The key to coming out is not fighting with the natural; it is fighting with the spiritual. If you use natural tactics to fight a spiritual battle, you will lose. In the middle of this fight, God will strip you to make the fight, appear to be unfair. Oh but don't despair God is a good God and **"His ways are not our ways and His thoughts are not our thoughts."** God knows how to fight the good fight for you. **"The battle is not yours; it's the Lord's."**

No matter what, stay in the fight by praying, praising, and worshiping God. You must be stripped naked of the natural and clothed in the spiritual. Naked my dear you came into this world and naked is how you get out. You must allow God to be your everything. Learning to balance both the natural and the spirit is a must.

We are all sinners saved by grace. Know that in everything that you do God is in it. He is right there to pick you up when you fall, and if you allow him, he will also carry you. I humble myself before the Lord, and I ask Him to allow me to stay in His arms. I ask for Him to walk with me in His arms. Yes, Lord. He is faithful, faithful, faithful. Thank you, Lord, for all you've done for me. It is easy when we are in the midst of our storms to forget that we serve a God that is the Almighty omnipresent, King of kings. **"He will never leave you nor forsake you."**

When in the storm we feel unworthy of the love of God because of what is happening or because of what we have done. Now is the time to hold on to God with every fiber of your being. God is the only one who can and will bring you out of this. So don't get angry with those who aren't by your side or leave you when the storm rages. God is just revealing to you that those that are not with you are against you and that your trust should always be in Him and only Him. Those nay-sayers have no power.

You must overstand that God has anointed you for a time such as this and that you will make it if you don't quit. It's alright to fall, but it is not alright to stay down, you must get back up again. Nothing fails but a try. Remember that for every failure there is a success, no matter how small. We tend not to count the small things as milestones. We look at them as meaningless, but that can't be further from the truth. It is the small things that become mighty in our lives.

When you can see the blessings in the small, it magnifies your faith. **"Faith is the substance of things hoped for and the evidence of things not seen."**

You have to be able to see past your circumstances. So what, things may look bleak to the natural eyes but when you look at the spiritual, those things you no longer see. That's what happens when you exercise faith. You have to hold onto the positive and focus on what God has shown you about your life.

Sometimes it's best not to share your dreams with others because those people can be negative. You surely do not need that in your life whether you are in a storm or not. Your faith is just that yours and your dreams are just that yours. Knowing this and keeping it in the forefront of your mind is a must. Not all will be supportive of you, even those closest to you. People fear what they don't overstand. As you grow stronger in your relationship with God some of those around you will start to challenge you and become angry even about the positive change that they see in you.

It's strange how those that are supposed to be for you can turn out to be totally against you. Be mindful of those around you, for your enemy is closer than you think. Getting to a place of solitude is not an easy task when you have encountered abuse. That comfort zone that is supposed to be there normally is no longer there. As hard as it is, you must find a way to get back what is gone. What so many others take for granted, often we that have encountered abuse yearn for, like a good night's sleep! Which is very difficult to accomplish when the body is living in constant fear because of that which has already happen. What is deemed normal for other's is not for us.

However, you must as a child of God find a way to grasp ahold of the faith and let go of that fear.

« 4 » LEARNING TO LIVE AGAIN

HAVE YOU EVER GOTTEN to a point in your life where every day you woke up seemed like a chore to get out of bed? Where there was nothing that you had to look forward too because your mind and heart, was so clouded by the pain. Where it was literary too hard to live. I have been there many times. I use to be too ashamed to admit even that to myself because I at that point was blaming myself for the cruel mistreatment. It is normal to feel this way.

My spirit was so low that I had to pretend to be okay because I knew that no one would overstand my pain. Pretending became my blessing and then later my curse. When you get good at pretending, those around you tend to think that you have it all together. They attribute this to what they think is a strength or someone who has no problems. Which we know that is as far away from the truth as the moon is away from the earth. You have to realize that there will always be people who have their perception of your life. There is nothing that you can do about that.

However, getting to a point of not caring what other's think of you and your situation is a must. That is the only way that you will be able to cope fully with and eventually come out of this mess.

Learning to love you fully is the most powerful thing that you can do for yourself. Self-love is the catalyst to breaking the chains that bind you. Once you give yourself permission to love yourself wholeheartedly, you will start to see things clearly. It will give purpose, to your life again, meaning to your suffering, and validation to your healing.

Expect to have those days when everything seems hard. When every aspect of your life reminds you of what you did wrong. Remember that this is normal. If you happen to be suffering from depression, anxiety, post-traumatic stress disorder because of the abuse, coping can become very difficult especially if you do not have a support system. Yes, God is always there. However, every soul needs to be connected to another. The human experience can be totally amazing when it is done right. To connect with the people, that God designed for you to connect with makes life bearable.

It is my hope that no one suffers in the ways in which I have. However fruitless as that may sound, it is sincere. Fear is the opposite of faith, and unfortunately, when abused, you live in constant fear, and that hinders your faith. You always have to remember that there are some things that you can't control. There are two forces working in your life. One is always working for you, and He is the Almighty

God, and there is one who is always working against you, and he is Satan.

There will always be both positive and negative forces operating in your life. It is called balance; one can't exist without the other. However, keeping this in mind will help you to overstand yourself and to cope with the course of events that may come up in your life. Difficulties will arise, but if a situation comes up and it's complicated, then it is not for you because difficult, and complicated are not the same. Difficulties require hard work for completion.

You must pay close attention to the events and people in your life that bring about complex events. It is never to be complicated. **Complicated is defined as: consisting of many interconnecting elements; intricate, involving many confusing aspects.** God is not the author of confusion. Therefore, Satan is. So no matter what event or person, do your best to stay clear of people and events that confuse you. It is a trap of the enemy. I have seen many people on a popular website use this term and to me it is sad.

These people have no clue as to just how serious this is by even using the term complicated. Complicated simply implies that you are confused about the state of your relationship. I can't stress this enough, get out of confusing and complicated situations before they cause you irreparable damage.

A person who refuses to define your relationship with them is dangerous to you in every area of your life. On the flip side of that is a person who defines your relationship verbally but doesn't follow through physically.

Talk is cheap and fruitless if it has no action with it. For instance, saying I love you and not showing it has no meaning. Always remember that love prioritizes, it is not optional. When faced with a difficult choice always keep this in mind. When someone loves you, they will never treat you as if you are less than or an option.

Love is the essence of your being and love demands to be placed first because my dear love is God and God is love. God will never take a back seat to anyone or anything. In learning to live again, you must learn to call on the name of God. Taking in the knowledge that He has one name but many titles and it is okay to call upon Him by whatever title that your heart wants to call Him.

There are so many who would get caught up in one title when God is multi-faceted, and one title can't even contain who He is. No matter past nor present the name is of great importance, however, the titles are where we get caught up. We tend to forget that we are created in His image and likeness, therefore, just as we are individuals who have different titles such as female, woman, daughter, sister, wife, mother, friend, teacher, etc., so does God. So your title for Him may be different than mine, but that doesn't make your title for Him wrong for you.

We as a whole must stop placing boundaries on who God is by getting stuck on what to call Him when we are in need. Let your Spirit lead you and not man. Knowing the truth is key. God wants us to call upon Him no matter what the situation or occasion is.

We must examine the word given to us by man and then ask the Almighty to be our clarity. In early biblical times, there were not vowels in the alphabet. In Hebrew God's name was spelled YHVH/YHWH, this is the unutterable name of God composed of the Hebrew letters Yod, He, Vav, and He.

He wrote HIS name with HIS finger. He wrote His name standing upright not side by side. He wrote His name with His flesh and bone. We think we know but do we? The YOD (the head), HE (the arms), VAV (the torso), HE (the legs). He is the source, the energy, the absolute essence of all beings, the great I AM. We are HIS IMAGE and HIS LIKENESS. Look at the written name as it is. It is a body; it is the body, the embodiment of who we are and who's we are.

We are and have always been filled with HIS SPIRIT, and until we come to that revelation, we will continue to be lost. There isn't a need for you to go looking for God because He is not missing. HE, IS, within you. From the very beginning when He breathe the breath of life into Adam He has been within us.

God wants us to walk this earth with the knowing of who we are and who we represent. With this knowing, you become an unstoppable force. You are then able to excel to heights that no one else has ever dreamed of because you have tapped into the God in you. The life force that has been trying to gain your attention for the duration of your life. Until you have accepted your path, you are merely existing. Once the path that God has chosen for you has been embraced and accepted by you, then the living comes. Now you can fully live as the oneness that you were meant to be. One with your mind, body, and soul. One with the Divine Spirit. One with you.

It is He who dwells within you not without you that is the author and the finisher. Nothing and I mean absolutely nothing that you have done, are doing, or will do has been done without His permission nor consent. He has been and will always be the watcher over you.

We are a part of The Infinite Source, and that Source is God "YHWH." We can keep debating about the correct way to pronounce and spell His name. We can even keep debating about what His name truly is or that the fact that the letter j was not a part of the alphabet at that present time, and it still would not change the fact that HE IS.

YHWH is the GOD of all gods. He is The Almighty God, that is who He is, and His name is YHWH, and He has many titles that permit us to call Him by many different variations of those titles, which equates to Him being perceived as having more than one name.

It is imperative that we allow our hearts to lead us when it comes to calling on the Almighty. Let the Holy Spirit lead you in all things especially when you are calling The Most High God. No one has a right to tell you which title is right or appropriate for you. YHWH knows your heart, and He knows why you are saying what you are saying. Don't keep getting caught up in the logistic of the matter just let the Holy Spirit flow freely.

When God commissioned Moses to be Israel's liberator from the bondage of Pharaoh's Egypt, he asked for God's Name to validate his God-given role to the children of Israel. God simply answered Moses, **"ehyeh-asher-ehyeh"** means **"I AM THAT I AM"** in the Bible.

When we sit and think about all that we was taught before this knowing about who our creator is, I have to ask myself was I taught the real truth? You know, growing up. It saddens me when I am in reflection, and I realize that I had been deceived whether it was intentional or unintentional, it was still done. That realization has caused me to seek and search for the truth that I need to serve better my creator.

Yes, I say, My Creator, because for me, this, whatever you want to call this, is a very personal experience for me for I am in a relationship with MY DIVINE CREATOR!

I have had to stop and reexamine that which I previously thought was the truth because it just didn't make any sense to me. I have since; I have been able to speak, considered just how important being silent is. To just sit and listen to those around me and then make my decision and or choice about what I have heard, learned, or even saw. One of those things is religion and what place, if any, did it have in my life.

I have learned that religion has nothing to do with who my creator is and that my creator operates in the realm of that which is spiritual.

Humans have branched out and created for themselves that which makes sense to them by forming groups, clicks, and cults to experience what they call religion. Religion, however planned, prepped, documented, or polished still has nothing to do with the very intimate spiritual experience of truly worshipping and relating to The Most High God.

As we grow in the faith, do we now realize that truth that we so closely related too is now in fact that carefully guided lie. Yes, I said GUIDED lie because once you come to the realization that the well-known truth was a fabricated tale, and you still do nothing to put the truth in a place where the lie existed then yes you are guiding that lie. Leading it in a sense to remain your truth, your reality although it is false and fraudulent.

Okay, for instance, the letter J was not in the Hebrew language when the Savior was born, so how on earth can His name be Jesus? What we as a collective whole have to overstand is that this Bible was translated from one language to another by more than one person and those that translated it did so with possibly good intentions, however, they were wrong about not just one fact but many because man does error.

So, therefore, since the letter J did not exist in the Hebrew language we can, therefore, deduce that many of the names in the Bible translation that begin with the letter J or has the letter J in them have been mistranslated. Which also leads us to wonder who, when, and how did all of this happen.

It is rather easy to believe a lie especially when BELIEVE always has LIE in the middle of it. Yes, L-I-E are the third, fourth, and fifth letters in the word believe, which spells out the word lie. So when you believe in something you don't partake actually in the truth for you must KNOW! For in believe there is always a lie in the midst of it. You at all times must overstand that it is either a KNOWING or NOT.

The fact is that you either know the truth or you know the lie. The knowing is the knowledge of that which is TRUE. Therefore, it is rather easy to continue to believe a lie than to acknowledge that the truth has been tampered with and that deception has played a key part in what you deemed to be your reality. Altered in a way that it creates thousands of years of discord and betrayal. The truth that has been layered with so many lies that it would take a sure act of God to reveal it.

With demonic tricks dressed as children of God, who are practicing agnostic occultism singing religious hymns and even carrying bibles in the name of who they call the creator. So then if a name is of great importance and as true children of YHWH who have been uttering the wrong name, then what does that mean for us as a whole. Especially when the scripture says that we perish for lack of knowledge.

The Creator has many titles. However, he only has one name (YHWH), and it is your prerogative to call upon whatever title you deem to be befitting for whatever circumstances that you may be going through at that moment and time in your life. You should also know the true name of the Creator and not just whatever title that you may utter at that particular moment.

It is said that the Creators Sacred name was lost in the translation because at some point in biblical times His name was only spoken at certain times and only by certain people.

I deduce that fear has created a massive mess, and as children of God we have to collectively as a whole figure out how to re-train our minds and bodies to follow our spirits instead of trying to force our spirits to follow us as human beings.

I can't say it enough, we were first SPIRITUAL and then natural. Therefore, the natural will never overrule the spiritual. Although it still tries because the flesh is weak and it wants what it wants. So there comes a point where you must bring the flesh under submission, and you do this by denying that which the flesh wants daily.

Denying the flesh is important especially when you are developing a deeper spiritual closeness and connection with God because it is through those denial periods that you are more in tune with His voice and His purpose in your life.

Learning to allow the spirit to lead is a must when working on the renewing of the mind. Most would like to think that the mind is where the spirit dwells but this is not the truth. The heart is where God dwells within you.

Therefore, the Holy Word says **"create in me a clean heart"** and that is what happens when God begins to dwell within you. God knows your heart regardless of the mind but also know that the mind must come under submission because the Holy word says, **"so shall a man thinketh so shall he be."** So, therefore, if you continue to allow the negativity to infiltrate your mind then those things will eventually manifest into the physical. So much so that our reality will become as dark and demented as our thoughts.

It is imperative that you replace every negative thought with a healthy positive one. So for every "I can't," there should be an, "I can". You must learn to be your own cheerleader, motivator, pep rally, etc. I know that you are wondering what motivation, and changing your mind and heart have to do with the name of The Most High God and my answer to that is everything.

You must learn to dismiss the untruths to gain the truths. Dis-spelling all the things that you were taught in the so called church that are usually done with good intent but are all the more wrong. See playing church instead of being the church is a trick of the enemy. There is a misconception that you go to church when in fact you go to praise and worship service. You are supposed to be the church, the body, the temple. See if you are going to it, and then that means you are not it. We have gotten so comfortable pretending that that very pretense has rendered the body impotent.

When being taught the word of YHWH you as His child should always be in safe keep mode. Safe keep mode is when you are retaining that which you are being taught. Studying the word of YHWH keeps you grounded and armed with the tools that are needed to defend yourself against demonic attack.

The Word of YHWH should penetrate your soul, rest in your spirit, and resuscitate your heart so that in times of trouble and doubt you have the assurance that everything is going to be alright because you are not alone.

However, if you are studying and being fed the proper spiritual nourishment, and you are not growing with your spirit, something is seriously wrong because you should not be regurgitating the word of YHWH.

There is a backing up of spiritual fluids which is causing the regurgitation of the spiritual food that keeps you in the infancy stages of spirituality. To vomit that which is best for you causes a spiritual imbalance that in turn cause a physical one. You are not growing in the spirit nor the natural because you are in an unbalanced state that has caused a weeping, and an oozing that has, in turn, created a physical and a spiritual sickness.

There's a gaping hole in the spirit that is yearning for

fulfillment that has you crying out of pain, and when the spiritual pain becomes so intense, it then causes physical pain. This physical pain can become extremely intense and even debilitating to the anointed one, and they may not even know why.

The yearning and crying out of the spirit to the flesh can also cause the anointed one to feel as though they are losing their minds and send them into a deep depression if this yearning is not fulfilled. See the spirit so diligently sends messages to the flesh to stop and submit and every time the Spirit does this, and the flesh refuses the spirit then causes the body to malfunction. Thus, the outcome is an illness or a DIS-EASE.

When the anointed one is in enough physical pain the cry out to YHWH is then used. There are times when The Most High God will allow attacks just so that we will submit unto His will. Yeah, I know that sounds rather harsh but when His choice is being resistant. He will for the greater good do whatever is required to place us back on course even if it's devastating to others.

This chosen path is never about the anointed one, it is always, and I mean always about YHWH. He uses people to do His will, to draw others that are lost unto Him.

At the very mention of His Holy name demons tremble and there is a shift in the Universe that aligns the things that have been misaligned. The natural course of things is nowhere near as important as the spiritual course of things. Always remember Spiritual first, then the natural second.

Again we are spirits housed in the flesh. Therefore, it is imperative that our spirits are fed accordingly because if it is not you will surely face physical ramifications. We become stressed when we are overwhelmed and are going against that which the spirit needs. When you cry out to YHWH, you allow Him the opportunity to pour fully into you in the manner in which is need to shift you back into place so that you can go further into His Kingdom.

When you allow the flesh to take over and lead, you lose valuable ground in your spiritual walk. The flesh must be disciplined and come into subjection to the Spirit for you to effectively do the will of YHWH for this life that you have been gifted with.

Every moment that you are on this earth must be filled with the anticipation of what is to come. The focal point should always be the outcome, the end results and not the present or current circumstances. If you kept your eyes on the natural event of things, then you are more than likely to burn out quickly because it is rather easy to become overwhelmed even for the anointed ones.

Daily meditation on the Word of YHWH should always be an important part of your life. Meditation keeps the physical and spiritual in alignment with one another creating the harmony needed to fulfill the task chosen for you by God.

« 5 » DISTANCE

SOMETHING AND SOMEONE HAVE to be let go. Change is a must in any healing process. I know all too well that change can be scary. We get content in our pain because sometimes it is all that we know and feel. Without it, we feel empty. That is the pattern of abuse. We even run away from anything that might just bring us joy and happiness because these emotions are foreign and all too unfamiliar.

Not having your needs met by the ones in your life can leave you with a feeling of emptiness, regret, and even shame. The feelings of rejection that comes from that can be overwhelming and leave you wondering, why? No one wants to be rejected. Rejection can lead to low self-esteem. It can also bring about insurmountable pain, anguish and eventually anger.

It is okay to be angry, but it is not okay to hold that anger inside. You must find a healthy way to release it. You must let the person know that their behavior is hurting you. It doesn't have to be physical to hurt.

Mental and emotional pain are just as bad as any other pain. No one has the right to cause you pain.

Selfishness is the catalyst to the majority of the pain that we encounter. When we allow selfish people into our lives and set ourselves up for defeat. I say this because you can't change the behavior of another individual. Selfishness is a choice.

When in a healthy relationship you will not encounter selfish behavior because each party is busy doing what is required to ensure that their part of the relationship works. Being selfish is a silent killer to any relationship. Putting your needs before that of the other is selfish.

When in a relationship the most important aspect is to know that there is no I in We. You are no longer single. You must learn to operate as a unit. The Bible states that, **"the two shall join and thus become one."** You must learn to make sacrifices and to compromise. It is no longer just about you.

There are certain behavioral traits that are learned. Therefore, they can be unlearned. It is about making a conscious choice to prioritize what is most important and vital to the health, well-being, and success of your relationship.

No one should ever be made to feel as though they don't matter, and everyone should know what it is like to both give and receive love. There are many people out there that do not know how to receive. Yes, that's right, they do not know how to receive.

That is called unbalanced. You must be able to do both.

There comes a point in your life where your giving should be reciprocated. The bible says, **"give, and it shall be given unto you. Pressed down, shaken together, and running over."** That means, in an abundance, not just a little bit.

It is okay to expect love in return for giving it. It is okay to wanted, to be desired. Those are natural and all so human. However, those are more importantly spiritual as well.

You should never have to question a person's love for you. It should be as apparent as the nose on your face. Love is felt even if it is never spoken. You can see love in the way in which the beholder looks at you, touches you, yearns for you. Love is, multi-facet and luminesce; it craves to be added too. It is a magnet that can't contain itself. It is not temporary. It draws you into itself and most importantly love is not selfish. Love and hate can't occupy the same space.

One would think that this would be apparent, however, for some it is not. I have heard many times that love hurts and this is not true. Love heals, builds, adds to, shows compassion, sacrifices, and love is above all else Godly. Love feels the others pain before it is apparent. Love gathers a solution before there is a problem. I have also heard and still do, **"what's love got to do with it?"**, and again my answer is and will always be everything.

Without love, there is no presence of God. He is and always must be the beginning and ending to everything in your life because if He is not in it, then Satan is. The bible states that, **"you can't serve two masters, for you will love one and hate the other."** Therefore, no space is completely void; it is always being occupied by something even if it is only air. You can however foolishly think that there is a middle ground to everything but there is not. You can't have good without bad, up without down, right without wrong, in without out, love without hate.

I have learned in my spiritual walk that although things may not have always turned out the way in which I have wanted, they still turned out the way in which God wanted. His ways are not our ways and, His thoughts are not our thoughts. I can't stress this enough. We do not and will not ever have the capacity to think nor even function as God does.

In His omnipresent status, He is everywhere at all times, watching and waiting for us to acknowledge, need, and want Him. He doesn't just exist; He is. He is already in the midst of everything that we do. However, He would love for you to want Him there, to even summon His present.

See every human emotion we have is first spiritual. Those emotions keep us connected to who we were and are first, and that is spiritual beings who just so happen to be operating as human beings with a physical body.

We are all multi-faceted cores of energy waiting and

wanting to be dispersed in a positive manner. When I say, "we all," I am speaking regarding God's children. The Bible states that, **"God knew you before, He formed you in your mother's womb."** So, therefore, that means that you existed somewhere else before now, even if it was only a thought in God's mind.

I am not going to get into a long drawn out argument about reincarnation or the afterlife because you do have a right to think whatever you want. My mission is to be of service to those who want to be in a positive relationship with God and who want to know Him as the love that He so clearly is.

Love is and will forever be the key to healing and even fixing a multitude of wrongs. God can do exceedingly and abundantly above anything, that we can even, hope, dream, or even think of. There is absolutely no wrong in truly loving someone. However, it is not feasible to love another being and not love yourself.

Distance is the prerequisite to healing whatever heartaches you have. Taking a step back will allow you a better view when trying to analyze the situations that plague you. It is okay to do this. It may not take long to see the light at the end of the tunnel.

Sometimes we are too close to the situation to clearly see it for what it truly is. Depending upon how bad your situation is, distance may just require going in another room, to the movies, a walk on the beach, or a trip to another town. Just know that when leaving home, again depending upon the circumstances, you may not be able to return.

So preparation is key to whatever distance you may choose and you must also take into account whatever consequence that may arise because of it. When dealing with the abuse, you should never, ever stay in a situation that may cause you bodily harm. Remember love does not hurt.

It is okay to cry. Crying is a release, an outpouring of emotions whether they be good or bad. Holding in hurt is a sure way to cause physical illness. Give yourself permission to scream and cry if you feel it is necessary, to your healing process. Sometimes I cry.

Whatever you have to do to ensure that your safety and well-being is intact is paramount. Always listen to your inner voice. That is your voice of reason; it is there to keep you safe. It is an internal alarm that goes off when you are in danger. Please adhere to it and never second guess it. Your body tells you when something is wrong. Listening to it will keep you out of harm's way. I can't even count the number of times that I didn't adhere to my internal alarm and found myself literarily fighting for me life. I second guessed myself because it didn't seem logical that the person lying next to me would do me like that. I was literally sleeping with the enemy.

The point that I am trying to make is that no one is exempt from disaster and betrayal, even the gifted. God doesn't show us everything. However, He does give us just enough to kept us from total annihilation. I am at constant odds with myself about this. I often wonder with the anointing placed upon my life, why do I still make the wrong choices? Why isn't my life the way that I want it?

Well, I have learned the painful truth. Gifted and Anointed does not equal to being The Almighty God. I am not God! I am however His child and, therefore, I know that there are certain things that I am going to receive simply because of this fact. Oh don't misunderstand me, I am not arrogant, I am just sure of who I serve and what that entails as, His daughter.

All of my prayers have been answered, and those answers are one of three things; yes, no, or not right now. Oh, don't be surprised, God does say no to His children, and He does make us wait on certain things that He feels that we aren't ready to truly receive. No, I don't have the full overstanding of how and why. All I know is that He will never leave us nor forsake us. I know that He loves us beyond measure. I know that all things work to the good for them that love the Lord. I know that my latter days will be better than my former days.

I try to keep in mind that even God will step back for a moment and watch. He is even sometimes silent but it doesn't mean that He is not listening, nor does it mean that He is not there.

Distance can be a very healthy thing and the prerequisite to curing what truly ails us. Just make sure that you do not stay away too long if you are trying to mend a relationship because too much time away from your spouse is a sure fire way to kill the relationship.

On the flip side of that do not go back to an abusive situation after stepping away because it will only get worse.

Time away breeds contempt in that abusive partner and please know that they are out for revenge. They will do and say anything to get you to come back so that they can fulfill their secret promise to themselves to finish you off. Their minds are not healthy, and you can't rationalize with an insane, sadistic person under any circumstances, so if you were blessed to come out of that, please stay gone!

« 6 » CONTRADICTION

I KNOW THAT THERE lies within us, at least, three different facets that make us who we truly are. Some people joke and say me, myself, and I. However, I am inclined to think that this is a very real possibility. That we all somehow are walking contradictions of the person that the people around us get to see. It is only when someone that you allow close enough to you that these contradictions reveal themselves. It is, however, a very real part of being human. There is the part of us that we present to the world, the part of us that we present to our friends, and the part of us that we present to our families. We reveal ourselves according to who the individual is that we are communicating with at that moment in time.

We as human beings are multi-facet and ever changing. We change according to our environment. It is also called adapting. That can be either good or bad. We have the ability to be interchangeable. If put into a hostile situation we automatically go into protect mode, survival mode, fear kicks in as we assess the situation at hand.

We are taught not to lie but if a situation arises that warrant us to lie to protect ourselves we will lie. I used this as an example because it is the simplest form of contradiction. We are all contradictions. It does not matter how large or minuet it is.

Whether you have taken a vow to be faithful, pro-choice, non-violent, if given the right or wrong circumstances, you will go against your beliefs, character, upbringing. We would all like to think that everyone goes by the book no matter what but even in the bible there are contradictions. Moses was a peaceful man but given the right circumstances, he committed a murder. David was a king who had many wives but became an adulterer, murderer, and thief. Thomas was a disciple of Jesus, walked with Him, knew Him to be the Son of God, but he still doubted Jesus.

I could go on for days about the biblical contradictions but I won't because you get the point. There are many situations that could arise to throw us off course and get us to go against our very nature. It may be sad to some, but it is the truth for many.

I have cried over this very thing many nights and days even, wondering why do I do some of the things that I do when I know that it is not right. As a little girl, I didn't dream of being rejected by my parents. Nor a latch key kid at 2. Having a drug addicted mother, raped at six, homeless, hungry, pregnant out of wedlock, cheated on, beaten almost to death, having abortions, suicidal, etc., you get the point, and this is only half of what I have gone through in this lifetime.

I am even saddened at the mere thought of this as I type. Seeing this on paper makes me feel horrible. I have been my worst enemy. I have allowed things to happen to me that shouldn't have because of my disobedience to God. No, as a child, I had no control over what other's did to me, but some of the things that I chose to do as an adult have been my fault. I take ownership of that.

No one on this earth can even fathom the pain and regret that I feel even to this very day. It has scarred me for life. I am guarded because of it and refuse to trust because of it. There are times that I don't even trust myself. Yes, you read it right. This anointed, gifted woman of God doesn't sometimes trust herself because of the mistakes that she has made. Yes, perfect Patty missed up! I tell truths that others won't. I screwed up, and I can't fix it.

I walk around every day filled with regret and shame with my head held high in public while screaming in private wondering how much longer do I have to live with this load on my back, this heaviness in my heart.

It's so sad that there is not one living soul on this earth that truly knows me! I have given so much of myself to others, but none has ever taken the time to give truly to me. I have even been told by several people in my life that it is because "you're strong, and you don't need it!" Wow, really? That right there is even a contradiction. Who on this earth doesn't have needs just because they are strong? I have been punished because I am strong when I am strong because I have to be.

No one has ever had my back, front, nor sides, except God. I do not know what it feels like to have someone fight for me, sacrifice for me, nurture me, even truly care for me. I am what I call a bottom feeder. That's a person who always gets someone else's scraps. A person who always is last. A person no one wants. A person who is only needed to fill in for someone else. You know the temp. So I hold my head high and fulfill the needs of others while my needs go unmet. I help people accomplish their dreams while mine merely stays a fantasy.

I have tried a lifetime to break this cycle, these unseen chains that bind me but to no avail, I still fail. My childhood traumas and experiences have left me scarred. I try to cover the scars, but they keep poking through to the surface whenever a fresh betrayal comes along. I pray, beg, and even plead with God to remove this burden from me but my answer is always, my child, not yet.

It is these scars, that push me to write, to sing, to think, to read, to hope for what should rightfully be mine. Forgiveness of self for failing and true love and acceptance of others. A person that has never been rejected can't even truly comprehend the pain that I feel.

I am told quite often that I do not know my abilities nor power. That I often look at my failures but never once stop to look at my accomplishments. Well, that is because of my contradictions. I do not see my accomplishments as accomplishments because it didn't turn out the way that I planned. For every lose I see as a failure. It is a shame that one's life doesn't reflect who they truly are on the inside. I am judged by what others think I am because I never have allowed anyone the proper access to the real me. Who just so happens to be vulnerable, afraid, battling depression and anxiety, riddled with guilt, suffering from multiple physical illnesses'.

However, on the flip side of that I am very funny, love to sing and very good at it, have a fondness for antique cars, love, love, love the ocean, and I am quite the adventurer and researcher.

I often wonder if I will ever allow anyone to see that side of me. I often deem most people that I am in contact with unworthy of such a gift, and I don't say that to be cocky or arrogant it is simply a fact. I am guarded and always have been, and the people who have entered my life have proven me right. So I stay guarded. Does it mean that I am hurt any less, no! Then I know that you are wondering then why, do I do it. Simply because it allows me to feel safe and somehow in control of my destiny.

My hope is to open your eyes to the contradictions that I have so that it will enlighten you to the contradictions that you have. It is okay, and it doesn't mean that there is anything wrong with you. You are simply human. We all war within ourselves, it is for lack of a better word, natural. There are however, those that would like to think that they are in some way perfect. Which is laughable because we are all imperfect people living in a perfect world.

I so desperately want to bring every facet of my beings somehow together in harmony, so that the contradictions don't keep me from conquering my fears. My number one fear now is being hurt by those that I care about.

I fear people, and I have become a recluse. Those that think they are close to me don't even realize it, and that makes me sad. They look at me as this strong, independent woman, who doesn't need anything nor anyone. Obviously, as you read, you have learned that is not the truth. Everyone on this earth needs someone and something. I am not sub-human, I am not a superwoman, I am not a robot!

You would think this would not have to be stated. That this is even obvious but on the contrary, it is not. There are those that just so happen to think this madness to some degree or another, which is disheartening and sad. I am the way that I am because of my experiences. I have had to endure horrible things at the hands of others, and I had no choice in the matter. I wanted to survive so did what was required. So if that makes me strong in the eyes of others, so be it.

If I could have done things differently, yes, I would have. I don't know of anyone in their right mind, who would want to be abused, tortured, rejected, and so on. However, life doesn't give you do over's or a magic time remote to rewind things. We have to play the hand that we are dealt and deal with what comes our way and pray that it is good.

I have analyzed every area of my life trying to figure out why and what I could have done to prevent some of the pain that I have inflicted upon myself. I try to research everything about me. I need to know what makes me tick. Why am I the way that I am, and so far my findings have been eye opening and amazing to say the least. I now have a better overstanding of some of my qualities and personality traits, but I still have not even scratched the surface of who this intelligent, wounded, multi-faceted, spirit-filled woman is.

I have a long road ahead of me and still plenty to learn about myself and why certain things were allowed to happen to me and what makes me the greatest contradiction in my life. I want to finally get to a point where nothing truly bothers me. A place where I can smile, and it is always genuine. A place where I don't brace myself or even expect hurt from others. A place where I can truly let go and let God. A place where nothing matters.

« 7 » Is it Really?

IS IT REALLY SIMPLE to just let it all go? To release, all of the hurt and pain? I have been trying to find a way to completely do this for years. I tried using the pretend method. You know, act as if it didn't really happen. It was just all a bad dream is what I would tell myself until the pain became so intense that pretending was no longer an option.

There's something cold about acting as if an event didn't take place in your life. Especially one that's so profoundly bad that it changed the very essence of who you were inside. Same face and name but totally different being. I often reflect back to the day that everything I knew was the truth changed for me. I found myself trapped in a world filled with rejection, distrust, anger, betrayal, and strife.

I was no longer the little girl that nobody paid attention too. I was now the little girl that every evil force wanted to strip away from all humanity. I was now damaged beyond repair. A child left wondering what just happened to me and why? I was suffering in silence for almost 20 years because of it. I still have not figured out until this day, why? I find myself often pondering over the events and wishing, hoping, even praying that I could just undo what was done to me.

I have heard many times that what won't kill you will make you stronger. That is one of the biggest lies ever told! Just because an event didn't take your life doesn't mean that you are stronger because of it. What it means is that you simply survived. I am so very tired of simple minded people whitewashing the truth. Just give it straight, no chaser. It happen, and it made me an even bigger prey for all the predators out there. I became this magnetic, a beacon if you will for the evil that sought to devalue and destroy such a precious gift given by God.

I was never looked at as a blessing by my parents nor was I shown any love by them. I now painfully overstand why but the overstanding comes at a price for which I had no way of paying.

There is something about pain that makes you feel hated and tormented by it. It is the catalyst that leads you unfortunately down a road paved with even more pain.

Scandal, I have survived scandal. There's a difference between a scandal and a controversy. **"A controversy is a debate, disagreement, typically when prolonged, public, and heated. Dispute - argument - contention - debate – disputation". "A** scandal is an action or event regarded as morally or legally wrong and causing general public outrage."

Can you get past me as the messenger and just get the message that God is sending to you through me, I am not perfect and never will be, I am flawed and have made many mistakes and will make more as long as I am wrapped in this flesh.

You can sit in judgment of me because of what you may think of me for the things that I have done. I am keeping it real, being honest about what I have done and who I use to be.

I am here to press pass the path that I use to be on and use my life as an example of who not to be and to show you just how good God is to me but allowing me to go through that and come out of that. I am still standing even if God is holding me up. It is okay because my Father sees me for who He knows that I am and not for what mere mortals think that I am.

My assignment here on this earth is not without controversy and I know that there are those who want to assassinate me. Wishing me dead and have tried to kill me. I am always on guard watching my back. I do not have a legion of friends and yes my walk is lonely, but as I excel in my walk with God, all the fake ones will be weeded out. All is well, and everything is under control. God is and has always been my way maker.

The sweetest revenge is not retribution it is my

success. You have to be careful about those that walk with you but are not willing to help you.

I thank you, God, for never leaving me and never forsaking me. It is okay that I was betrayed by those that claimed they love me because God has me covered and in my weakness he is my strength. It is my duty to serve. I am a servant of the all mighty God and I must at all times remind myself of this because it is very easy to feel as though being a servant is beneath me, but on the contrary, it's actually above, anything human, to be a servant of God.

I will not hide behind my salvation but stand on my testimony. I must in the midst of all of my hurt and pain, disappointment, and disgrace, still remember why I am here on this earth. It is simply to be a servant of God, to glorify and edify God with whatever gifts and talents that, He has filled me with and with my last breath I will praise God.

Whether contradictions, lack, disappointments, anger, betrayals, and all that come against me, I will still say, **"for God I live and for God I'll die. I will bless the Lord at all times, and His praise shall continuously be in my mouth."**

I am one of God's exceptions, and I am coming out of this refiner's fire shining as pure gold. What God has done for me he doesn't just do for anybody. It is not about being arrogant. I am just sure in whose I am and who I serve. It is the anointing on my life that keeps me in my right mind. It keeps me being different from the rest. I have been counted out many times, oh but my God has made me an exception and saved a wrench like me.

God has broken the rules to bless me. I have been left for dead and came out of that. I know what God can and will do for me. Oh sometimes I cry but sometimes those tears are those of joy because I know that I should have died. I know that it is the goodness of the Lord that has kept me.

I know what it's like to have no one, and nothing but I am here to tell that in those moments God has shown up and showed out in my life. He has brought me out of the most horrible situations and elevated me to spiritual levels that I never dreamed possible.

Financially I may not be where I use to be, oh but when I think of the goodness of the Lord, my soul cries out yes, Lord! Because of the anointing on my life, everybody in my circle that has a connection to me are going to be blessed.

I am getting ready to experience a radical breakthrough that is also going to bring my friends out that are suffering lack as well. God says that I am not to worry about the start because all I have to do is start it and He is going to finish it for me.

I started this book on faith while everyone around me was negative and doubtful but I am still pressing forward in the midst of naysayers and doubters. For the glory of God, not for me. It is to save the next woman that is getting ready to or already dealing with some of the things that I have already experienced. It is okay that you feel lost, alone, defeated, dejected, etc., but you will still come out of this. Your contradictions and doubts are just a small part of a greater purpose. You are human.

God wants us to make the first move, and He will do the rest. I know that you may be afraid. Step out on faith and see the goodness of God shine forth in your life. Break the spirit of procrastination over your life. Remind yourself as I do when I become overwhelmed that this too shall pass and that you are coming out. Feeling down is normal when you have gone through such horrible trauma.

I have learned that it is okay and to give myself permission to feel whatever emotions that may arise in my life. I have even started to acknowledge the pain that I have suppressed nearly all of my life. Oh, trust me when I say that the road to redemption hurts. It's like having surgery to repair something inside of you that's broken. Those of you who have never had surgery probably wouldn't overstand this analogy. When, you awaken from surgery, you are in more pain than you were before and you often wonder did I do the right thing because this is more painful than what I had. Simply put, it gets worse before it gets better when you are working on healing.

There are no quick fixes to healing a lifetime of the abuse, I know because I have searched near and far just to come up empty handed. I have even prayed for a magical moment where all of the abuse, pain, and torture would just disappear. Well, that prayer was answered, but unfortunately, the answer was no. I had to suffer through the process. Again gifted and anointed doesn't mean, exempted! You can let go and let God, but just know that doing so doesn't magically make everything disappear. It just means that you trust that He will heal the broken places in your life, if you are willing to go through the process.

« 8 » PEOPLE PLEASER

I REALIZED THE OTHER day when I was having a conversation about my life and all that I had encountered that I became a people pleaser when I was a child. It first started with my mother. She wasn't around much, but when she was, I would try my best to be a good little girl so that she wouldn't leave me. It was my way of showing her that I was worthy of her affection and love. I so desperately wanted my mother to stay home with me, to just be there. She was all I had but she didn't want me. She never said it to my face but her actions told the whole truth and nothing but the truth. I was in her way, and nothing I did made her change her ways. I was a latchkey kid at two because she didn't have a sitter for me.

I was often left alone but she always made sure that I had sandwiches and juice in the bottom of the refrigerator before she left. I learned how to be alone early in my life because I didn't have a choice. Soon the spirit world became my family and friends. I do without a shadow of a doubt know the Holy Spirit and God's Angels. Without them, I wouldn't be alive right now. They were my comfort when I needed it.

I remember being a perfect Patty, always trying to do the right things. Overly helpful, you know to the point where if I tried hard enough, they would love me, keep me, stay with me, but that never happened.

I remember the first time that I was raped, my rapist told me at the age of six that he was doing that because I needed to be punished because I was a bad girl. That stayed with me for the rest of my life. I looked around at the people in my life and at the way they were treating me, and I saw that my rapist must have been right because if I were a good girl, then my mommy wouldn't leave me and my daddy would have wanted me.

So I went on a quest as a six-year-old to be the best that I could be so that I wouldn't be punished like that ever again. I made sure that I was quiet and didn't ask for anything. I stayed in a corner to myself when I was in the house. Outside I learned to climb trees and would stay there for comfort and food, plus it was safe. I couldn't get raped if I was high up in the clouds as I would say. Soon my method would turn on me, and I would find myself being taken away instead of left alone. I found out that being taken away was far worse than being by myself. Alone meant that no one could hurt me, being around people meant that I would be raped again. I was a lamb sent to the slaughter house.

It's something when you know what is going to happen but are powerless to stop it. I have been forced to endure some unspeakable things as a child, and no one cared enough to protect me.

Most children who are raped are raped without a witness. Well, that was not the case with me. I was set up by my very own aunt. She took me right to my abuser. So not only did I have to deal with the brutalization but I also had to deal with the betrayal of a loved one whom I trusted with my life.

That left me guarded for life, but it didn't save me from being abused again. The fact that I had a mother who wasn't watching me made me an easy prey for my predator because they are hunters. They sit back and watch and listen. They become close to the family of their next victim, even friends, if not already family.

Most children are already familiar with their abuser. These children are the loners, the ones that are already hurting from lack of attention or rejection.

I was a quiet, shy little girl that was different in many ways from those around me. That included looks and stature. I was ridiculed by the other children and the adults. Which more than likely contributed to me being chosen as a target.

Once a child is raped, they somehow become a magnetic for other predators. I have researched this extensively and still have not come up with the answers that I seek. I have grown tired of hearing, "why not you?" Well I say to them, "why not you?"

That is one of the most insensitive things I have heard in my life. Be careful, what you say to a person that has been abused in any way. Your words can kill that person's spirit. You are their link to life or death. They need your compassion, not your cynicism.

If we could just get over it, we would. No one wants to be filled with so much hurt that it literally chokes them. Those who have not been abused can't begin to fathom the constant torture that we go through. We relived every event that has caused us great pain. The smallest of things can trigger us to relive every moment of our torture. It can be a smell, color, sound, or person.

Those of us that have been abused get a life sentence because of someone else's sinister crimes, while most abusers will not do one day behind bars. However, do not give up hope because the God that I serve says that vengeance is His.

There's something to be said about a child who wants to please at all costs. I became great at being abused. Oh yeah, you read it right. I took my abuse and never told anyone. After being raped, I was given candy and told not to say a word while semen soaked my panties. The thought at this very moment makes me want to vomit! I thought I was peeing on myself.

As I sat on the passenger side of this car wishing that I was dead, my aunt and her man laughed and talked as if nothing had happened. I never overstood that day and I probably never will and yes, it still hurts deep down to the very fiber of my being, but I know that God still has me here for a reason. I know this because I have begged God to take my life, and He said, no.

I have begun the very painful task of healing and with that process, I am learning to be pleasing to God. I want so desperately to please God that it hurts. Oh, it is a different kind of pain though. I have not mastered it yet, and when I fail, I'm usually devastated. I am a work in progress, and that is what I try to keep in mind.

I want to live a life that is pleasing to God. I no longer want to be that little girl that tries with all her might to please a mother who detested me and I no longer want to be that woman who attracts all the broken men who look to me to spiritually fix them.

I want to be so filled with God that there is no more room for the pain. As I look back, I am humbled as I recall all the times where God has saved me. I know that you are probably thinking, saved you? With all that has happened, how can you say, He saved you?

The answer is simple to me, because God did save me and He is still saving me. God loves me so much that He wouldn't let me die because of the wrong. I am flawed, but He loves me, not in spite of who I am, but because of who I am. He knows me better than I know myself and loves me even with that knowledge. Yes, I went through unspeakable horrors, but I have also witnessed unimaginable miracles. I am a miracle. God has done and is still doing a mighty work in me. Yes, me!

This woman engulfed in pain, but also this woman filled with the Holy Spirit too. I do not know what tomorrow may bring, but I do know that I serve a God that does know, and I have to trust that, He will never leave me nor forsake me. I am not perfect, but a perfect God loves me. I will continue to push past this pain, and I will keep quoting, **"Philippians 4:13 I can do all things through Christ which strengthens me."**

As I run towards the mark, I will forever keep in mind that I am working my way towards being an avid pleaser of my Father whom art in Heaven. I love you Lord because you first loved me.

It is not a mystery that all of us at some point in time have done or said things that have gone completely against what we have been taught. It has also been times where we have also tried our best to be of service to someone who just didn't treat us fairly.

I am just trying to make those unaware, aware of the fact that you are not alone, and it doesn't make you weak nor foolish; it simply makes you human. Just know that as I continue my walk with God I am learning that I must first and foremost please Him and in doing so I am walking by faith and not by sight.

« 9 » TO THINE OWN SELF BE TRUE

ONE OF THE WORST things that you can tell yourself is a lie. It's bad enough to lie to other's but when you're the one, telling yourself lies that borderlines on sickness. I was an expert on lying to myself; there's no wonder why others continuously lied to me. They were only following my lead. It took me many years of my life to learn this, and it still makes me sad. It is a fact that we have all lied, but the sad reality is that a lot of people believe their lies and sometimes the lies of others. For whatever reason this reigns true.

No one truly wants to be lied too. Although the truth can be very painful, depending on what the circumstances are. This is a subject that most would rather not approach. Being lied to is a hard thing to face. Especially when it is someone that you love. Lies and betrayal go hand and hand. Lies can cost a person their life, but I am not talking about lying to save your life. Some lie so well that it has become first nature.

The truth is embedded so deep within them that they can't even dig it out. The sad reality is that they wouldn't tell the truth even if their life depended on it, so you know that your life doesn't stand a chance.

I had become accustomed to lying to myself about being abuse. So much so, that when I was forced to deal with it, it was as though I was trapped in someone else's life. No, not me I would say. I must be dreaming. Maybe it was just my imagination. Yeah right, it was me, no I wasn't dreaming, and it wasn't a nightmare, nor was it someone else's life.

The sad reality was, that was the only way that I could cope with the pain, and the betrayal of the act, was to pretend like it didn't happen. I tried desperately to forget but I just couldn't, so I lied to myself. I told myself that, that day never happened. I didn't overstand it nor did I know how to deal with such horror. So I internalized it and tried to go on.

By internalizing the pain, it allowed me to become a magnet for other abusers. Oh yeah, these demons have internal radars that can detect someone who has been brutalized and they horn in on that. Mind you these are predators, hunter's, if you will. Their mission in this life is to heat seek out whom they may devour.

There are those that think that I am melodramatic. Well, you can think whatever you wish but it is a proven fact, and it is the naivety of other's that allows these predators to continue doing what they are doing. Just because you don't believe in something doesn't mean that it doesn't exist. That is in itself another form of lying to yourself. I have tried repeatedly to overstand why certain things happen to certain people and not, others. Some would like to think that it is destiny. Other's would say that it is just a matter of being in the wrong place at the wrong time. Whatever the explanation is, someway somehow I need to know just for me.

There had been times when I tried so desperately to rationalize everything that has ever happened to me but, of course, it didn't work. There was no logical explanation as to why, other than the fact that I didn't have the proper caretakers growing up. Then if that is the case, what about the events that further traumatized me as an adult.

I learn the other day a very valuable lesson that I wasn't even expecting to learn just by putting to use my library card. I decided to take a break from everything and bask in the writings of one of my favorite authors. I did all the research and found the perfect book that would get my mind off of everything. I put in the order for the book and waited for the notification saying it's time to pick it up.

Well, I finally get the email saying I can pick up the book. So I go online to see when the library bus would be in my area. I mapped out everything, triple checked it all and headed out to get my book. Well, when I got to the location the library bus was not there. So I checked online again and made sure that I had the correct information. Well, I had the correct information and still no library bus. Now I am upset. I did everything right but still did not get the right results. So I start thinking what do I do now? So I remembered that I had the number and call them, and they confirmed that they are to be in my location but at a different time. So I go on to explain to them that their website lists their location and time differently that they told me.

So I informed them of the error, and they informed me of their exact location, which happens to be only two blocks from where I was awaiting. So I go and finally retrieve my book and head home thinking what just happened? Is this the answer that I have been praying for? Is this what I have been missing?

I did everything right but did not get what I was supposed to because someone else made an error, which caused a delay. After I had made it back home, I kept thinking about this. Then it dawned on me after having a discussion about it that I could apply this error to the questions about my life that I had been seeking. I had been right all along, and it wasn't that I had miscalculated or did anything wrong. It was simply that other forces were at work here. That someone else was holding up my blessings. That someone somewhere had made a critical error. I was at the right place, at the right time based on the information that I had received, which turned out to be incorrectly based on someone else's, mistake.

The point that I am trying to make is this. When it comes to blessings, other people are required to get them to you and if one person fails to do what is required properly then your blessings can be held up.

I am in a place spiritual right now where I feel stuck. I am wondering what happened because I am not supposed to be here. Spiritually I am supposed to be further along. I am at a place of uncertainty, and it hurts my heart to know that this spiritually gifted woman of God is stuck.

I am never the one who claims to have all of the answers but on the other hand, I am not an idiot. If I do not know the answers, then I do my best to find them. I research until I am sick just to get the answers. I pray to God, beg even for answers, clarification, wisdom, knowledge, etc.

I know that sometimes there just isn't a logical explanation to some of the things that happen in our lives but I would still hope someday soon that the logical could, at least, be explained to me. Is it really that difficult to get to the root of why these things happen to me?

I see others living and loving one another on this wheel I call life, and I wonder where on God's earth is mine? There are certain things on this earth that we all have a right to as children of God. I am afraid that I will leave this earth without having my needs met.

My spirit yearns and cries out for that which God says that I am to have. I am searching as the word of God says. **"Seek and ye shall find."** I have been seeking, and I have yet to find what I need. I require help with this task, but there is not one living soul that will touch and agree with me on this. I feel overwhelmed and at times lost because of it. I have prayed, fasted, and studied but still have not come up with any answers to my questions. I feel as though I am running out of time and that scares me. Yes, this woman of God is afraid. Yes, I know that God did not give us the spirit of fear. Yes, I know that His grace is sufficient for me.

I also know that my flesh is fighting against my spirit, and I am struggling to bring my flesh under submission with my spirit. What I state is not hypocritical, it is human. I am human. I know they say that the obvious need not be stated, but I disagree because sometimes the people around me seem as if they have forgotten that fact.

I know that something has to break loose soon, and I am bracing myself for it. I am thankful for all that God has allowed me to learn on this journey, and I am looking forward to my harvest. I do not know what tomorrow may bring, but I do know that it is in God's plan for whatever it is. I claim the goodness and the mercy, along with the grace of God over my life. This quest is one of purity, and my prayer is for God's ultimate fulfillment to reign in and over my life.

I know that I am different, and I accept that difference and I move forward. I know that Love is what God is for me, and I know that He will continue to reveal Himself to me. It is a given.

« 10 » REFLECTION

I SOMETIMES WONDER WHAT is it that has me in this dormant state. I began seeking this answer years ago. What I have thus far learned is that I changed from that which I considered to be the normal me. As I continued to press forward in my relationship with God I have learned that the things that I use to want I do not want any longer. My requirements have changed, and now I am seeking that which I know that I am worthy of. I know that God's word has transformed me in a way in which, what I deemed to be good is no longer that for me. The desires of my heart have taken me to another level. That which use to satisfy me no longer does.

I am not afraid to acknowledge that I am a new creature and old things for me have passed away. I want what God's word says that I can have, and I will not stop until I get it. I am in expectation mode. Every day I awaken to the knowledge that this is the day. Anticipating what God has promised me. Praying for it to manifest in the physical. Speaking those things that are not as thou they were. I am claiming my rightful place. The inheritance of my Abba in heaven.

I can feel my manna coming from heaven. I don't know when but I know that it is on its way and soon. Some would deem this as being cocky, but I know that it is blessed assurance. The word of God says that I am and will, so I take that as a fact. I know that in the physical, things look rather bleak for me. Oh but just keep watching and see the manifestations of the Lord reveal themselves. It is just a matter of time for me. I can never say this enough, it is okay to expect and anticipate your blessings from God.

As an heir to His throne, you have that right, and nothing nor no one can take that away from you. God wants us as His children to know our rightful place. It is a must because you can't truly operate in the fullness thereof if you do not know who you are, or rather whose you are. Take heed as to your position in the kingdom for it is paramount to the path that is chosen for you. You must search and seek out all that is required of you. Study to show thyself approved. Never allow any other human being on this earth to know you better than you know yourself.

Learn what and who makes you tick. What and who changes your mood and feelings towards yourself. As children of the Most High God, we must be careful of those that we allow to have control over our emotions. For moment to moment while wrapped in this flesh those emotions are continuously shifting. Our emotions can even stop us from hearing from God if we allow them. I know firsthand about this stronghold. Some would say that women are overly emotional creatures. Well, I am not going to either confirm nor deny this. All I am going to say is that we as human beings are all emotional creatures.

Those emotions can quickly get out of hand when we are dealing with those that we love the most. See it is through those that we love the most, that our ability to be hurt is greatest because we have our guard down. Those are the people who know the most about us, such as our strengths and, unfortunately, our weakness. However, you have to stay prayed up and hope that the Almighty power of God operates in your life so that this never becomes a factor.

It is a very difficult task to operate in an emotionless state because as a human being we are emotional. Yes, we are first spirit beings who happen to be housed in a natural body. Therefore, the natural body does desire what the spirit sometimes does not. We are in a constant battle with our flesh as spirit beings because it is through the flesh that the enemy attacks us first because he knows that our flesh is weak. Although the word of God says, **that "we wrestle against not flesh and blood but principalities and rulers of the darkness."** This is because it is the underworld or shall I say that it is in the spirit world where the war is being waged.

It is not just the seen that can cause you harm; it is the unseen as well. Most would like to think that the spirit world does not exist because for them it is easier to pretend that the unseen is a non-reality when that is far from the truth. Just because you can't see it, does not mean it is not there. The greatest harm to you comes from the spirit world. There are forces that try to condemn and control you. I have learned that sometimes no matter what you do certain things are just predestined to happen.

No, I am not saying that you shouldn't try to do the right thing. What I am saying is to do the best that you can do and if by chance things go in the opposite direction to that which you were hoping just know that God is in control. I often have to remind myself of that fact because sometimes I become overwhelmed when I have done everything right and for whatever reason don't yield the proper results.

It is a very painful realization when you have done everything that you were supposed to and come out on the bottom end of it all. I keep telling myself that **"through all bad some good must come and that the righteous availeth much."** I quote as many scriptures as I can remember at the times when I feel defeated. God always have a ram in the bush when things go to the left. Trust in the fact that the word of God says that **"we have never seen the righteous forsaken nor his seed begging bread."**

Do not get discouraged. Hold onto God's unchanging hands. Use your time of reflection as an example and analyze both the good and the bad. Look at what God has brought you out of and at what He has blessed you with. His grace and mercy reign in our lives. He is a just God. I have made a lot of mistakes and some of them I am yet to overstand, why? I still cry because of them and wish that I could take them back. I have prayed many days to God for overstanding and clarification. I prayed to be one of those that truly, I mean really and truly have no regrets and not just say it.

For I know that most who say that they have no regrets are no being honest with themselves nor others. That's like saying you have never sinned, done anything wrong, nor hurt anyone. We as human beings do fall short and it is okay but being in denial about the shortcomings can be disastrous. Admitting is the first step to healing. I take ownership of that which I have done, and I am a work in progress still searching for ways to right the wrongs in which I have done. I know that I also have to be realistic when it comes to change for everyone is not receiving of your apology.

Not everyone will forgive you, so you must prepare for that. There is always a chance for rejection. Righteousness and holiness do not guarantee that others will be receiving. Even the word of God says that **"all will not be saved."** I have learned that even the right decision can be a painful one. Just because it feels bad doesn't mean that it is not right. In all things I say do it with love because with love you can never go wrong. **"For love is God and God is love."** Remember that love has everything to do with it and real love can and will conquer it all.

So for those that say that love wasn't enough, have just said that God wasn't enough, and that scares me. See a lot of people confuse lust for love when the two are not the same. Lust in a temporary infatuation with someone. Oh, but love is everlasting and never ends. It is heartbreaking for me to know that I have caused so much pain to others throughout my life, especially when I was younger. It doesn't matter that I was young, what matters is that I did not operate in the will of God, and I will forever regret that.

I often wonder what my life would have been like had I truly surrendered to God when I was younger. I hear people often say, **"well it happened the way it was supposed to."** Well, that is not true because we can alter our course by making the wrong choices. Those wrong choices can cause critical delays in your life.

We sometimes go through unnecessary suffering because we made the wrong choices. I am truly guilty of that. Lord, how I wish that I could turn back the hands of time. I have delayed God's purpose for my life by being ignorant, selfish, and just downright cruel. Yes, I knew better.

We all know right from wrong, however just knowing is half the battle. We must exercise right judgment in everything that we do, and this must start early on. I have learned the painful lesson of letting go. I have let go of revenge, controlling others, selfishness, etc. for the purpose of healing.

Oh, yes, I still get hurt, yes, I still get angry, and yes, I still get sad, but I try not to allow those moments to revert me back to who I use to be. I keep in mind that, **"vengeance is mine saith the Lord."** This stops me from retaliation when I am wronged by someone else. Exercising restraint is paramount to walking by faith and not by sight.

It is very easy to allow the human side to take over when you are in pain. The enemy is at his busiest when you are hurting. It is his job to kick you when you are down and to point out everything that you have ever done wrong.

Some would think that just because you are saved by God's grace that makes you exempt to the troubles of this world. Oh, but don't be fooled because it does not exempt you or anyone else for that matter. We still go through, but the difference is that we go through with the full knowledge that God is on our side and that the Lord is interceding on our behalf.

« 11 » WANTING

I HAVE HEARD SINCE I was a little girl that patience is a virtue, but no one ever said what was the formula to waiting without wondering when. I have never been a patient person and waiting has always been hard for me. I want what I want, and I want it now. Well, guess what, it still has not happened the way in which I wanted it to, and I am still wanting and waiting.

It saddens my heart to know that what I have been wanting and waiting for I already had. I just didn't know it. It is a real shame when you are blessed beyond measure and don't even have a clue that you are. As I have gotten closer to God, I have learned just how blind I have been. As they say, **"you can't see the forest for the trees nor the trees for the forest."**

I have cried many days since I have decided to actively pursue God because I have learned that I have given away so many of my blessings because of my inability to know the spiritual value of just what I had. I went looking all around for what was already within my grasp, already within my reach. What do you do when you have failed to see that which was for you right in your face?, and now that you have thrown it away you can't get it back not even from another.

God only knows the pain that I feel from the horrible mistakes that I have made. I have been in a constant state of wanting for years. Walking around filled with regret and sadness. No one and I mean no one knows just how this has affected my life. As I work on my relationship with God, I learn just how messed up I am and that there is more work on me to do than I originally thought. I have learned to be brutally honest with myself. To examine and critique every area of who I am and hope to be.

"To thine own self-be true" is the quote that I think of as I write this because if you can't or will not be true to yourself then who can you or will you be true to? I am tired of lying to myself. I have begun the painful process of breaking down my own walls that I built to keep myself safe and from pain because that has been my false sense of security. I packed so many layers around me that even I couldn't penetrate them. It was that false sense of security that kept me from truly loving myself and from even being able to see when anyone else was trying to love me. Oh yeah, I am keeping it as real as I can. Even the word of God says that, **"the truth shall make you feel."**

I pray that at this very moment that whoever is reading this realizes the love that is in your life before it is too late and learns to be thankful for what you have and who you have. For tomorrow is not promised to you. Look around you and thank God for the simple things. Like the kiss from your spouse, the flowers that they bring, the bills that they pay or the attention that they give to you. These things are not automatic. Thank God that He sent you someone that loves you and learn to work through whatever small unpleasantries that come. Having good quality human companionship is essential to our very survival.

The human touch is important and studies have shown that it is the very link between life and death when dealing with premature and ill infants. Also, adults benefit as well, so don't take lightly the human touch. God designed us to be social beings, who interact and show compassion and love toward one another. We are the elite among the species but act as if we are the last on the gene poll.

We must take our rightful place and be who God intended for us to be. We have dominion, and it is time for us to start claiming it. Even monkeys interact and groom one another as a sign of love and affection, but we as humans act as if the human touch is unimportant and obsolete. It is truly a shame that most couples don't even hug, hold hands, nor kiss each other, not even during the most intimate moments of making love. Lord, I just don't overstand why our basic needs as human beings are not being met.

I have a longing, a wanting to have that which God says that I am suppose to have. Even the United States

Constitution says that, **"we have a right to pursue happiness."** So if man can say that and even put it in one of the most important documents in history, then surely God has trumped that by promising us as His children even more than that. It is our right to be loved, nurtured, held, touch, desired, etc. You have a right to want more than what you have, and it does not mean that you are selfish. It just simply means that you are operating in the fullness of the Lord by holding firm to His word that whatever we ask in His name we will have.

If you can conceive it, then it can be made so. We as children of God have the power to manifest whatever it is that we desire. God's word says that, **"He will give us the desires of our hearts."** I claim that in the name of the Most High.

God knows what we want before we do. He knows us better than we know ourselves. So stop listening to naysayers about what you will not get. They are not God and have no right to tell you what you will not have. God is the God of all things, and He can give you a thousand horses on a hill if He wants too. Stay away from negative people when you are praying to God to manifest your hearts desires because they can block and even delay that which God has awaiting you.

Everyone that says they are for you are not, just as everyone that smiles in your face isn't your friend. We as God's children must learn to discern between those that are for us and those that are against us because the enemies can very well be in your midst. The importance of agreement is paramount in coming out of and obtaining anything in the kingdom of God. The word of God says that, **"one can chase away a thousand while two can chase away ten thousand."** I am constantly looking for those who will touch and agree with me.

It even breaks my heart when I know that those that are close to me do not trust in God's ability to transform things in my life. I often cry when it is revealed to me that most of them are fake and are praying for my failure. Oh yes, everyone that prays for you are not necessarily praying for goodness for you. Be careful of those **"hope she gets ran over by, a truck, prayers."** We would love to think that all that are around us are for us, but that is not the truth. We must learn to accept that fact quickly.

However, just know that God has you covered and He has placed a ram in the bush for you. I tell myself that often because I find myself always caught up in a situation like that. To the point where I am so closed off that it hurts. I try my best to protect myself by being introverted. I often pray for God to guide people into my life that will add to the goodness, who will be for me and not against me. Those that deeply love me for me and truly want what is best for me. It is disheartening to come to the realization that the people who you help want to harm you. I am so tired of crying about betrayal and loneliness.

I know that I am just one person away from my breakthrough and every day I get up with the anticipation that I will meet that person who will help propel me into my destiny. I have learned that it is not time that transforms or propels you; it is a person that God has assigned just to you to launch you forward. I have researched until I was sick trying to attract that individual to me. I have prayed, fasted, asked questions, etc. and to no avail, I have failed to attract that person.

No, I don't know who it is or where they are, but I do know that somewhere out there is someone whom I need to be of help to me. I need help! Yes, I am screaming it from the top of my lungs. I am not even exempt from begging if I have too, this is deeper than wanting your nails done or your favorite pair of jeans.

I want the promise of God to manifest in my life. I want the promises and dreams that God have shown me to manifest themselves into the physical. I have seen it in the spiritual; now it is time for it to be seen in the natural. I claim it, right now Lord, in your name.

« 12 » HONORING THE POWER OF TWO

It is said in the word of God that, **"one can chase away a thousand, and two can chase away ten thousand."** With that being said one is powerful, but two is far more powerful. The power of agreement of two children of God can change many things. Honor protects, corrects, submits, and listens. We all must choose to honor someone at some time in our lives. Honor is a seed, and it should be sown in a matter befitting it. When you make the choice to honor someone it is not a sign of weakness, honor is a sign of strength. There can't be a price put on honor for real honor is priceless. When we as children of God speak His word, we are doing so with expectation. It is okay to expect the manifestation of God when we, **"speak those things that are not as though they were."**

The word of God is powerful and when we honor God for His ability to manifest His word into the physical we are showing the ultimate faith. For **"without faith, it is impossible to please God."** God loves when His children exercise faith in His ability to manifest His word into the natural. Some, of course, say that this is foolish, but that is not the truth because **"God is a rewarder of those that diligently seek Him."** God wants to know just how must you trust Him by asking for what you desire of Him.

The word of God states that, **"He will give you the desires of your heart."** See, God doesn't just supply you with your needs but He will give you your wants also. What you want is a desire. God wants you to be faithful to Him; He wants you to know that he is able.

I often ask God to surround me with people who can elevate me by teaching me that which I do not know. I am not intimidated by those who have more knowledge than I. I am rather intrigued because I see that as an opportunity to learn more. I thirst for knowledge, like a dehydrated athlete, thirsts for water.

I am continuously thinking of what I can do to increase my faith. I study the word and recall as many scriptures as I can. In times of trouble, I call on my fleet of warring Angels. I summon the Holy Spirit. I acknowledge the Holy Trinity.

The point that I am making is that I do whatever I have to do to get past that moment of doubt. Some would like to think that when you are saved by God's grace that you do not have moments of doubt, despair, or even confusion.

When you become saved, it doesn't mean that you are exempt. I have said this before, and I will keep saying it until you get it. Becoming a servant of God means that you take up the cross and follow Him. You will suffer in His name just because you have made the choice to serve. Only the naïve think that it is a magical potion that takes away everything bad.

God has all power, He can do whatever He wants, whenever He wants, however, he wants. He does have the ability to transform in the blink of an eye, however again it is His choice. I know that, **"through all bad some good must come."** That no matter what happens God has me covered.

Do I want to go through some of the things that I do, no! But do I want to be who I use to be, no! I am on a continuous path of spiritual growth. Every single day I am evolving, transforming, changing, and becoming who I am to be in Christ. I thank God every day and I honor Him by working towards being who I am supposed to be. Does it mean that I am perfect and without sin, no! However, it does mean that I am comfortable enough in my relationship with God to say**, "Father forgive me for I have sinned and fallen short of your glory."**

God loves me, this I know for the bible tells me so. Yes I still sing this in my times of sadness and despair. I know that I am loved by the Father, the Son, and the Holy Ghost. My Holy Trinity, without whom I am nothing. I give honor and praises to them, for without them I am nothing.

Oh God, I thank you for loving me enough to show me who I am in you. I am the daughter of the King and an heir to the throne. I am saved and accepting responsibility for who I am and what I've done. I know that without a shadow of a doubt that God loves me, and he knows me. **"He knew me before He formed me in my mother's womb."**

In my frustration, I have said and done a lot of things that have gone against the will of God on my life and for that, I will forever regret. Some would say that I have not been patient or that it is not my season. Well to that I say, miss me.

See the power of two is one of the most powerful unions on earth when done in the will of God. That is one of my frustrations with my life. Yes, I am going to say it. I do not have my Divine partner in the natural. The man that God created just for me and only me. I have been told by naysayers that I am too picky or that he doesn't exist.

Well, I serve a God that says otherwise because He is the one who put this desire inside my heart. I want what God says that I am supposed to have, and I am doing everything that I can to ensure that I am ready when he arrives.

Yes, I operate in Divine order and yes I do know that God loves me enough to manifest what He says that He would manifest just for me. No, I am not cocky nor arrogant. Like I told you before I am being assured. I know what my Abba told me. So when you try to place a seed of doubt on my blessings, then I have to eliminate you from my life because I need those who will touch and agree with the word of God on my life. I do not have time for doubting Thomas's.

The power of agreement is a mighty thing even the word of God says so. **"Where two or three are gathered together, except they agree, I shall be in the midst of them."** That's what the word of God says, and I know that to be the truth. You have to find someone who agrees with the dreams that God has placed inside of you. It is vital to the manifestation of whatever God chose for you to do.

No one and I mean no one on this earth can make it alone. God's word even says that as well. It is not good that man should be alone. It is not healthy to be isolated, lonely, alone, without love, companionship, the human touch. We all need those things to survive.

Christ even stated in the word of God that someone touched Him and virtue left His body. It was the woman with the issue of blood. She knew that if she could just touch the hem of his garment that she would be made whole. She didn't even have to touch His body. She knew that all she had to do was touch His clothes. If that is not a clear indicator as to how powerful the human touch is, then that's like saying that God isn't real, and I know that He is. That's why it is imperative for me to be with my Divine Partner.

As I grow closer to the Lord, I know that the men that I use to allow in my life weren't worthy of me. I need my man, my Divine partner, who knows God and who

God knows. The one who will love me like Christ loved the church. The one who will die daily for me. The one who looks at me and knows that I am his wife and the way that he obtains favor from the Lord. The one who gives me his 100 percent knowing that he will get the same in return. I am not afraid to say what the Lord says that I am worthy to have. I do not care if you don't know my value. I am the daughter of the King, and I know what He says that I am to have. I am now operating in the fullness thereof, and I will not settle for less.

The man that God prepares for me is Divine and royal. His heart beats to the same rhythm as mine, and he thinks of me just as he thinks of God for he knows that we are created in God's imagine and likeness. He is my protector, my confidant, my prayer partner, my lover, my friend. He is as I am. We are one and the same, just as the word of God says. **"The two shall join and thus become one."**

Yes, I am claiming what God says is mine. Move mountains for me Lord. Make a way out of no way. Oh, glory be to El Shaddai. I know what I know, and I am what God says that I am. I will not allow any more negativity to cloud over my joy. I will not allow anyone to filter negativity and doubt into my thoughts. My God said that, **"my latter days will be greater than my former days,"** and I claim that.

I will do just as the word of God says: **"Seek and ye shall find, knock and the door shall be open unto you."** I am going to do whatever I have to do to allow the manifestation of God's blessings to reign in my life. I know that I am just one person and the Divine appointment has been placed on me. Just as I know that El Shaddai is my one love, and He loves me so much that He sent His only begotten son to this earth to die for me. Yes, for me! Christ was sent here to die for me.

I am and always will be amazed at that fact. God did it for me. God made a way out of no way, and He will send my Divine Partner to me because He knows that I require a human companion on this earth to be of help and service to me as I march forward on my chosen path while basking in His glory.

Oh, Lord, I thank you and magnify your name. I operate in the fullness of who you are, and I will not allow anyone else to tell me what you will not do for me. Every day that you allow me to wake up is a day that I will glorify and edify you, Lord. I know that without you God I am nothing and with you I am everything.

I have missed out on so much because I was running away from that which was for me, out of fear. Oh, but Lord I will not run away no more. I will stand on your word and know that you are my redeemer. I will continue to diligently seek you, Lord. I will hold firm to what you said that I am to have and to be. I will not continue to allow that which is not of you to consume me. For I know that You are right here with me, carrying me through whatever storms, trials, tribulations, and obstacles.

Thank you, Lord, again for saving a wretch like me! It

is through you that I am made whole, and I know that before I even finish typing this sentence that everything that you have shown me in my dreams, all that goodness has now been manifested in the natural. Thank You and to God be the glory.

« 13 » EXPECTATION IS MANIFESTATION

NO ONE IN THIS world wants to be alone nor lonely. These two things are devices of the enemy to break your spirit. God even said in His word that, **"it is not good that man should live alone."** With that being said I want you to know that healthy long-term relationships are important to who we are in Christ. When you are working on getting closer to God through a relationship with Him, it is important also to stay close to people who have knowlege of the Holy Ghost because you are doing the Lords work and coming into contact with unsaved people. So there must be a solid foundation for you to go back to to be replenished. Helping to bring the unsaved to Christ is demanding and draining. It is not easy, but it is our job as ambassador's.

There are those moments when you will be sad, alone, and confused. Just keep in mind that these are devices of the enemy and get out of these moods as quickly as possible. Love is the key to whatever troubles you. That is, even more important to keep in mind. Whenever you encounter negativity, hurt, pain, betrayal, etc. just know that God is able and get as close to someone who truly loves you as quickly as possible because that is where your restoration is.

I say it often God is love and love is God. When you keep this in your mind, then you will do what needs to be done as quickly as possible. You must stay focused on the positive and use affirmations continuously. Words do matter that's why the enemy wants you to keep dwelling on all the negative, bad, and demeaning crap he throws your way. One of my favorites when I am struggling is **"Psalms 4:13, I can do all things through Christ, which strengthens me."** I repeat until I feel better. I focus on what God says that I am to have.

When you are chosen, it is never an easy battle, but please keep in mind that if it were easy, then everybody would do it. This walk with God always comes with its challenges, and that is why I hold fast to the scripture that says, **"for we walk by faith and not by sight"** because if you focus on solely what you see, then you are doomed.

The enemy loves to use the negative things that we see to try and discourage us. To try to make us think that God is not real. Oh, but He is real, and He loves us, and He is working on our behalf even when it doesn't look like it. **"Faith again is the substance of things hoped for and the evidence of things not seen."**

So just because you don't see Him or the thing that you are praying for doesn't mean that God is not there pulling things together for you.

You must seek someone who agrees with the dream that God has placed within you. Someone who will encourage you when you can't encourage yourself. A person who truly trusts in God and His abilities and will pray for you as they pray for themselves.

Oh yes, it is possible because God says so. The word says; **"seek, and ye shall find and knock, and the door shall be open unto you."**

Do not listen to people who say that things will simply work themselves out because that is not true. Remember, **"faith without works is dead."** You must be willing to do what is required to make whatever it is that you want to work. Nothing and I mean absolutely nothing happens without some effort.

The power of two is totally phenomenal. When you agree with another human being, it changes things not just on a physical level but also on a spiritual level. The power of agreement was created by God so that we will know that we require help, and it is okay to do so. Stop thinking that you can do everything by yourself. Even Christ, our Savior, required help carrying His cross. Why? you say, because it was an example to us.

For as long as you are a spirit housed in flesh you will

need assistance from another human being on this earth. So stop the independent crap and fall on your knees and ask God to send you the person that He designed to be of assistance to you. Also, make sure that you are open to whomever He sends. I have learned the hard way that sometimes your package may be wrapped differently than you had hoped. However, it is what's behind the face that matter's the most. The spirit that the body is housing is the fruit of your prayers.

"Seek ye first that the Kingdom of God and His righteousness and all these things shall be added unto you." You know the sad part about writing this is seeing the error of my ways. Seeing how many times I have delayed my blessings because I didn't like the wrapping on the package. Even now I have to say, Lord; please forgive me. It is something when you come to the realization that things are messed up because of you.

Now I have to work even harder to get back to where I need to be because I foolishly took the long way around. My prayer is that someone out there can learn from my sufferings and not make the same mistake as I have. Please heed my warning. Be thankful for what you have, especially the love in your life because baby everything that glitters is not gold. Trust that God, has you covered and know that no relationship is perfect. Remember that, **"the race is not given to the swift but to those that endure until the end."**

Communication is the key to working out all

problems. We all must learn how to communicate effectively with the people in our lives especially the ones that we love and that loves us back. That creates a stronger bond. Holding back only causes anger and bitterness to fester and grow, this leads to feelings of inadequacy and eventually shutting down.

Everyone needs to know that there is someone on this earth that has their back, no matter what. No one and hear me now. No one on this earth was created to be alone. There is someone out there for you. Someone who was created just for you and only you.

Oh, Lord God in heaven, it took me many years to learn this. Unfortunately, my lesson came with a great deal of pain and suffering. If you don't get anything else, please get this, you are worthy of the type of love that God says that you are supposed to have. That's right, I said it, supposed to have. No one on this earth can make it without love.

The first and most important love of all is the love of God and then the love of self and then the love of others. You will know love when you feel it because it takes over you. Real love adds to you. It doesn't take from. It builds and not tears down. Real love is not painful; it does not hurt. Real love is God.

It took me many years to learn what human love is because I didn't grow up with that kind of love. I even doubted God's love for me because of the horror I had experienced at different points in my life and yes I doubted the love I even had for myself at some point as well. Oh yeah, I know you're thinking, how dare she say such a thing. Shame on her. Well guess what I am saying the things that are required to save you and I am telling the truth.

Oh, I know that the self-righteous ones never had moments like these. Not! It is my honesty that makes some people hate me, and that is okay. Can't please them all and I am not going to try. Only God knows the things that have hindered my purpose, and only He knows the struggles that I still have to go through, but I will not give up. I will still keep pressing forward. God does not require that I be perfect, He just requires that I trust in Him and have faith that He will do what He says that He will do.

Perfection is not and has never been a goal of mine. My goal is to keep pressing towards the mark that God has set for me. There are many things that I still do not overstand, and I may never get all the answers that I seek, but I trust that God has me covered and that, **"He will never leave me nor forsake me."** I know that there is power in two and that unity is a must. I know that there is more good going on in the world than people are willing to admit.

I also know that there is someone walking this earth that was created just for me. I know that when God looks down at me, he smiles and not in spite of the who I am but because of who I am. I know that I am the daughter of the King, and the things that I have done does not take away from that fact because my Abba knows my heart. He sees me in a way that I haven't even seen myself yet. I know that I am created in His image and His likeness. So that means that every time I look in the mirror I am seeing my beloved Father.

It is not with arrogance that I speak but with assurance. I am what and who God says that I am. I can look back on a time when I was afraid to say that because I didn't think that He would love me because of all the wicked things that I had done to myself and especially to others. But as I grow closer to Him I learned that it is not by deeds that God loves me, but it is through, His grace. I am so very thankful for His grace for seeing past my faults and loving me according to who He is.

I know that I am not where I want to be, but I also know that I am not where I use to be either. I still have plenty of work to do, but I am willing to do it. I now know that I am worthy of all that God can and will give to me.

I have had some major setbacks, but I have learned that those were just set ups. God has allowed certain things to happen to me so that He can get the glory. I trust that He will always get the glory in all things. His word even says it. **"Through all bad some good must come."**

I wake up smiling now, knowing that, **"this is the day that He has made, and I will rejoice and be glad in it"** because what He has for me is for me.

« 14 » CHRIST NOT KARMA

I OFTEN THINK ABOUT how is it that we say, **"what goes around comes around,** and everyone says, **you know it's karma."** I have been guilty of that as well. However, as I began to truly pursue a relationship with God I learned that karma has nothing to do with Christ. See the word of God speaks of, **"when you take up the cross you become a new creature and old things are passed away."** So that means that whatever you did before you submitted yourself to the will of God has no barring, on who you are now.

The word of God also speaks of forgiveness. That if you ask God to forgive you He will. Therefore, the old has nothing to do with the new. God is a forgiving God, and I have to trust in that fact He is a keeper of His word.

It is the enemy that tries to get us to think that we are not worthy of forgiveness, goodness, and love from God. This is to keep us trapped and bound by our mistakes. He knows that if he can do that, then we will never operate in the fullness of the Lord. Daily I have to keep telling myself that I am worthy of all that God has for me and that, **"no weapon formed against me shall be able to prosper."**

I constantly speak the word over my life especially when I am feeling down because the enemy doesn't fight fair. He will beat you to death when you stumble because he knows that you are at your weakest point.

He will not wait until you stand back up because this is his advantage point. That's why we as children of the Most High God have to remain prayerful, **"for we wrestle not against flesh and blood but against principalities and rulers of the darkness."** The enemy operates under an entirely different code and being fair and just is not in his game plan.

We must remember that our words and thoughts are very powerful, so we must learn to control them quickly to ensure that we are grounded. This is why **"we must study to show ourselves approved."**

"Satan is a thief and his job is to steal, kill, and destroy." God, however, is the giver of life, the builder, and the restorer. I often sit back and over analyze everything about me, my life, and those around me. To me everything has an answer and nothing is a coincidence. It is all a carefully designed plan by God even the pitiful mistakes that we make. God knows what we will do before we do it. I know that there are two roads to everything in life, and I sometimes think we as human beings often take the long way around.

It would be great if we could just get it the first time and go straight to it. Oh, don't get me wrong some of us are blessed to do just that. Not everyone takes the long path, unfortunately, for me, I am not one of them. My path has been long, hard, and very painful. I often think of what it would have been like to have chosen the shortest path.

I imagine myself filled with the love and laughter that joy brings. I smile at that fact that on the shortest road I wouldn't have made any mistakes. I would have had the most fulfilling relationship with God from the very beginning. Oh, wait a minute, as I am typing this God says you have my love always had the most fulfilling relationship with me. I am even now thinking back on some of my earliest conversations with God when I was a small child.

My point with that is just because we sin, fall short, make bad judgment calls, errors, etc. doesn't mean that we don't know God. It simply means that we are human beings housing a spirit being. Our mistakes are a part of us being human. Oh, but our ability to call on our Savior for forgiveness and know that we will receive it makes us spiritual. To know that no matter how many times we fail God is there if we truly trust Him and He will restore us, and make us whole again.

No, I am not giving you a reason just to do whatever you want without regard to the laws of God. What I am saying is if you mess up, He will forgive you when you ask Him.

We serve a God who is compassionate and loving. A God that created us in His image and likeness. A God that is omnipresent. Wow, that right there made me smile to know that He is the great I am, and I am His, created by Him and for Him. No matter how many times I say it, it is always new to me. I am in Christ, and Christ is in me. I love that even in my nothingness God has chosen to still, love me. He nurtures me and comforts me.

He tells me that my past has no barring, on my present nor my future and that karma has nothing to do with Christ because He died for my sins. So what I will reap is all the goodness of the Lord because He sowed His life for me. I have been bought with a price, and Christ paid that price for me. I choose to trust what the word says and I will continue to walk in that. I know that the victory belongs to God, and I know that as long as I am clothed in this flesh that I will error. I will still continue to serve God and repent and trust that there is light at the end of my tunnel. Even when facing the most hurtful and negative of circumstances I must keep in mind that God is in control, and he knows what I need before I do.

There are moments when I struggle to overstand some of the things that are going on in my life and at these times I cry, pray, research, study, meditate on scripture, etc. to get through that moment. I know that through studying the word of God and actively seeking a relationship with God that karma has nothing to do with being born again.

It is so easy to fall for the hype of man and question

the will of God. God's ways have nothing to do with mans, ways. God does not always deal with the logical ways in which we as people see things. He deals with the possible and what man deems the impossible. He is the maker of miracles and the creator of himself which is love. He tells us that whatever we ask in His name it shall be given. He also tells us that when we truly repent and ask for forgiveness, then those things that we have done are no longer remembered by Him. So that blows a hole in that karma theory. Yes, I know that you are thinking well what about **"you reap what you sow."** Well yes, you do reap what you sow when you don't truly turn those negative things over to God.

Christ died so that we may live and, therefore, you do not have to keep sitting around waiting on karma to slap you in the face because of past sins or mistakes because with God all is forgiven when you ask. Karma is a trick of the enemy to get you doubting the love and power of God when it comes to redemption, renewal, restoration, and forgiveness.

« 15 » SELFLESS

CAN YOU? YEAH, YOU. Can you be selfless when it comes to loving, living, giving, and being? This is a very simple question but yet has a very wide array of complexities. When first asked most would say yes, but most of them mean no. We as human beings base most of everything we do or know on a condition, although very few will admit to it. For instance, when entering into a marriage the vast majority do so because their spouse has vowed to be faithful, loving, responsible, and trustworthy.

Well, what happens when all of those are taken away from the relationship? Will you still be faithful, loving, responsible, and trustworthy even when the spouse has decided not to? It's easy to claim to be selfless when the person that you are making the claim to is doing the same. However, most people on this earth are selfish. Wanting what we want, when and how we want it, with very little regard to what anyone else thinks or feels. Oh, but we serve a God, who continuously shows us His selflessness because He loves us when we disappoint Him. He even still provides for us when we don't give Him any of us. The scripture about the prodigal son is a perfect example of a father's selfless love towards his son who left home and disappointed him.

The greatest gift that you can give anyone on this earth is your selfless love. The love that the scripture speaks of. No matter what another human being says or thinks of you, love with your whole heart. Love the way in which God intended for His children to love. Without question and fear. Love is the greatest of all commandments. Therefore, it should always remain first and foremost in your life. When you love, and I mean really love, you allow God to transform.

For the word of God says that, **"God is love and Love is God."** I have made a vow to love the way that God intended for me to love because through doing this I open up my heart to also receive love in that same manner because the word of God says, **"give and it shall be given unto you pressed down, shaken together, and running over."** Yes, Lord, teach me.

It is through the power of God that I sit here and type the words that He gives me because it is never by my might but by His. I am utterly amazed at his love for me and words can never fully explain all that He has instilled in me. Although it is His will that I try to tell you about all that He has done for me. My soul at this very moment is overwhelmed because of His goodness as I reflect upon just how much He loves me.

There is nothing on this earth that can compare to the love that God has shown me. I am not speaking of the human love that we show towards one another but the agape love that God shows no matter what I do. When I do not feel worthy, He touches me with His spirit and lets me know that everything will be alright. It is through God's selfless for me that I see myself as a better person, and I have begun to forgive myself for the pain and anguish that I have brought upon myself being disobedient to God. It is a very painful realization when you come to the conclusion that most of the things that you are going through, are a direct representation of the poor decisions that you have made.

Some would like to blame it on life, but 90 percent of it is self. Don't get me wrong, there are plenty of injustice's that happen to ordinary people, this is not what I am speaking of. The choices that we make causes us one of two things, joy or pain. Your happiness should always be the goal when making any decision. It is okay to want the best for yourself, and this is not selfish behavior.

Being selfless is about the true giving of yourself for the betterment of everyone around you, but not at the expensive of your happiness. It is through your happiness that others are supposed to be filled with happiness. True happiness is contagious, and those in your life should be happy about your happiness and vice versa.

Making the choice to love with your whole heart is the most selfless thing that you could ever do for anyone especially yourself. Being selfless in the spiritual sense has nothing to do with the man-made definition of the word. Being selfless does not mean that you take no regard for you. Selfless from a spiritual standpoint means that you removed the human and allow the spirit you to take over. The God in you steps forward and starts to operate in love when dealing with the people you interact with. No, it is not easy to let go and let God when you are accustomed to operating with your earthly self. It is a daily quest and one that should not be taken lightly.

So many are on a quest to find love, so much so, that they forget to look within themselves first. You must become what you are looking for before you attract what you want. Study yourself. Ask questions. Be honest with yourself about what you want and why verse what you need and why? Make sure that you are in alignment with God and consult him about what is best for you because His presence and guidance in your life are essential.

« 16 » SPIRIT VERSES THE NATURAL

DOING THE RIGHT THING is not always easy. If it were everyone would do it. This fact is not about judging. It is about the reality. As sad as some situations in life can be we as children of God must find a way to push past all of the pain and anguish we feel when others wrong us. Surviving is not living. Just doing enough to get by is not succeeding. The journey starts with the true determination to press past all the negativity surrounding you. To lift yourself higher than the meaningless expectations of others. It is the true self that needs to break forward in order to live in a place that is only meant to be temporary. Freedom is breed from allowing the Holy Spirit to reign in your life no matter what. We must learn to live every day as if it were our last.

We as human beings fight against our spirit being because we don't overstand how to truly let go and let God. We are taught that we are to respond to the things that we can see and are not taught by our caregivers that it is the things that we can't see that are the most important.

As children, we are taught to be seen and not heard. Our voices are silenced before we can even speak. Constantly being told that if you can't see it, then it is not real. Having us doubt the true power of the Holy Spirit and, therefore, doubting who we are as spirit beings. Disrupting the anointing placed on our lives and causing great pain in our growing process, which will eventually lead us to make disastrous mistakes that we would not have made had we been armed with the truth. We struggle when we get older and become afraid of the gift of the anointing because we were not allowed and taught that it is a part of whom we are, God's children.

It saddens me when I look back on my life when I tried to seek help when my gift started to manifest itself and was told to shut up and don't speak of that again because people will think that you are crazy. Forced to hide the gift and forced to suppress it, causing yourself unimaginable pain and anguish. Walking around afraid, confused, and dejected. You become isolated and alone, wondering how and why this is happening to you. Leaving scars on the soul. Chopping off bits and pieces of your spirit. Wondering if you are crazy as they say. So you start to create your own world. Operating in this unseen reality while trying to be what society calls normal, but normal to whom? What a bunch of crap, there's no such thing as normal. We are all different people trying to cultivate and operate different personalities in the same manner while pretending that it is okay.

It's not okay, and no two human beings are the same, just as no two spirit beings are the same. We must start teaching the truth about who we are and whose we are before it is too late. Our children are the future, whether for the good or the bad. They are the soldiers of tomorrow and we must instill in them whose they are and who they serve before the enemy recruits them.

You can sit there and pretend as if Satan doesn't exist and watch your children go to hell in a hand basket or you can get off your butt and start equipping them with the tools that they need to be productive in this battle. Our children must learn the word of God while they are yet young. Don't what until they are older to start instilling the word of God in their hearts. Read it to them until they can read it to themselves.

It is the denial of our spirit that keeps us bound. The blatant refusal to accept the fact that we are spirit beings first and human second. Don't confuse what I am saying. I am not telling you to try to suppress the human side of you because that is an impossible task because we need our bodies. What I am saying is to allow the spirit you to lead the natural you. This will enable you to have a better overstanding of who you are and whose you are.

There are times when the challenges we face hinder the spirit from functioning at its full potential. Being overwhelmed and bombarded with so much negativity can lead to feelings of hopelessness. It is a must to be surrounded by positive people who can build and uplift you especially during those difficult moments. If those that are in your circle can't be of support to you, then you need to reexamine those in your midst. It is imperative that you are surrounded by people who have your best interest at heart.

Greatness requires a team to achieve the goals that God has placed before you. No one can excel without excellent people around them, pouring into their cause. No one and I mean absolutely can make it in this world alone. It is imperative that we overstand that it is natural to require help and to want to be connected to another human being, the ones that God designed for you. I am so very honored to be in the presence of God, and I know without a shadow of a doubt that He will never leave me.

During our walk on this earth, we will sometimes get discouraged, but it is not life that have the twist and turns, it is people. Being connected to the wrong people will kill the dream that was placed within you.

I have yet to overstand fully the path that I'm on, but I know that God is carrying me. I am not walking with God; He is literally carrying me. I could never walk this path without His legs, His strength, nor His will. I am very special to my Heavenly Father, and I know this because of what He has and is carrying me through.

There are moments when the seed of doubt tries to plant itself, and I have to hold firm to what God has placed within me. So I have to speak the word of God to myself for, **"I am more than a conqueror and no weapons formed against me shall be able to**

prosper." If it were not for the will of God in my life, I do not know where I would be. It is a shame the mess that I have made of some of the things in my life, and I know that it is God that keeps me moving forward and trusting in the dream within me, even when all looks lost. At those times, I quote, **"I must walk by faith and not by sight."**

It is the vision that we see in the nature that can hinder our spirit. It is the power of perception that makes and even breaks us. It is the joy and the pain that makes us who we are. The success and failures are a part of us all. Being a child of God does not make us exempt from being human.

Humans are flawed, but in Christ, we are made flawless. The trials of life build character in the human part of us. God wants to see us operating in Him by loving when all else seems to be failing. To reach beyond our humanness and reach within and draw on the spiritualness. Love is healing for the body, redemption for the soul, and connection for the spirit. Without love, we are empty, hollow, and devoid.

The spirit man existed long before the natural man did. So the need to have the spirit man recognized is a must to whom we are in the natural. We have to take the time to nourish our spirit just as we take the time to nourish our bodies. We spend so must time working on the natural that we neglect the spiritual part of us. We are connected to the greatest power source, and somehow we tend to forget that. We do not plug into our source enough to get fully charged, which leaves us quickly drained when something natural comes against us. It's like having a smartphone that has all these programs running in the background that you are not aware of. Well, these background programs help the smartphone function properly, but these programs also require a lot of battery power. So although the phone may be in your purse or pocket appearing to be dormant, it is still in use. The battery is working hard to keep all the unseen programs running so when you decide to use a program, it is all ready to be used, but if you don't keep an eye on the battery power, the phone will use up all the batteries supply leaving the phone useless.

Well, that is the same thing with the spirit and God. You must plug into your source several times daily to keep functioning at full capacity because of all the things that are operating in the background secretly using up your spiritual supply. Without the source which of course is God then you the body housing the spirit is rendered useless.

« 17 » THE POWER OF SUGGESTION

THERE IS POWER IN the thoughts that we have, and there is, even more, power in the words that others try to turn into thoughts that we have. For instance, constantly telling a person that they are worthless, soon they will start to think that. The mind is a very powerful thing and when used correctly can take us to heights that no one else thought possible. However, on the flip side of that, it can take us to lows that no one even deem possible.

The word of God states that, **"so shall a man thinketh then so shall he be."** Our very own perception can shake and break us or mold and make us. It is how we view ourselves that dictate who we are and sometimes the perception of others can do the same.

The wrong person can have you spinning out of control with fear, doubt, confusion, and even self-loathing. So it is imperative to be careful of who you allow in your head, space, zone, domain, etc. For everyone that tries to enter don't have good intentions.

I have learned to ask myself when someone enters my life, "what are you here for?" There is always a reason. They are either coming to build or tear down. To love or to hate. There is no middle ground to it, for even the word of God says that, **"you are either for me or against me."**

We as children of God must be mindful of the way in which we treat people because they may be assigned by God to bless you. God will also bless those in your life because you have been chosen to break all the strongholds and demonic ties from your family, just because you are in it.

We in the body must overstand that we are already under contract or shall I say covenant, with God. However, the enemy would like you to think otherwise. You must know that God has already touched you. He doesn't want no demon in hell or walking this earth to touch you. God even says that in his word, **"touch not my anointed."**

I must state again that everything that God is telling me to write must be and will be lined up with His word. The scriptures are here as a service to you who may not be familiar with the word. We as His children must continue to arm ourselves with Scripture so that we will be better equip to resist the enemy in times of attack and make him flee.

The enemy is clever when it comes to twisting and

bending the word of God, and the only way that you will know that you are being deceived is if you are also armed with the word of God. Knowing who you are and whose you are is only half the task. You must also, **"study to show thyself approved."**

It is through supplication and prayer that we can better overstand what it is that we should be doing and who we are. We are to learn through studying the word of God how to think of ourselves as He thinks of us. God has a profound way of instructing us on what and how to do the things that He has assigned to us. He also teaches us through His word about how our words and thoughts can either make or break us.

He has even shown us in His word how even he has thought and called forth things. Being our God, he has set a standard for us and teaches us by example on how to be, and what to do. At the beginning of the word, He simply says, **"let there be light,"** and it was. He was showing us how powerful we are, as we are created in His image and likeness. So, therefore, we too have the power to call forth things as well. However, we must first know that we can. He also tells us that, **"if we think that the mountain can be moved, then it can."**

It is through the process of learning whose we are that we can finally identify with what we can do as His chosen. God wants us to be confident in who we are in Him. To know without a shadow of a doubt what He has placed within us. We have dominion over everything on this earth. We were created for a time such as this. It is through the power of suggestion that we can either be made whole or broken. As good as it is, it also can be just as bad. Be mindful of who you let speak in and over your life because everyone that enters your life is not there to build you up. They are without a doubt sent; there's no questioning that. The question that should and must be asked is, who sent them? Listen, Satan has his hell's angel's assigned to you as well. He has set a team in place just to try and disrupt the path on your life. It is up to you to determine whose team the newcomers are sent from.

Keeping in mind the facts is a good indicator of discernment. Okay, it is a fact that, **"Satan has as many children as the seas have sand."** So with this fact, you know that everyone that approaches you is not a child of God. So with this fact, you can further overstand that everyone that enters your life do not have your best interest at heart and are not there to make your life merry and pleasant. No, they are not going to all tell you that, but I have a twisted respect for the ones who will shout out that they aren't meant to bring goodness into your life. Oh, don't be shocked! There are some demons that will reveal themselves with the hopes that you are too busy, overwhelmed, preoccupied, or religious to know the truth. Yeah, I did just say that. Again religion and spirituality are different.

You can be so busy ushering in the ministry that you forget to read your Bible. You forget to pray to the God that you claim to be ushering for when we know that you have made the pastor of the congregation your God. By doing everything that you can to please him and forgot that you are to be doing what is required to please the Most High True and Living God! You have gotten so caught up with the man of the cloth that you forgot that it is the spirit of the man you should be concerned with. Are you truly there to receive divine instruction or are you there to seek approval from the man that stands before you asking for your tides and offerings?

Don't misinterpret what I am saying, yes, you are supposed to give. However, you are also supposed to receive. Ask yourself, are you being spiritual fed or are you partaking in a side show for entertainment purposes? You are to be in a place where you are being spiritually taught how to be in a relationship with God. Sometimes this requires you to be corrected and guided but not babied and told everything that you want to hear just to get you to give. It is time out for play worship.

The time has come for us as true ambassadors to get on the grind for God. To stomp down doors for Christ by working harder on becoming a better servant. You must be mindful of whom you worship with because everyone in this service is not there to get closer to God. Some are there to do the devil's work. Oh yes, there are demons in the pulpit and the audience. These people are set in place to confuse you. They use their messages to deter you from the true will of God by twisting and bending the scriptures to fit their own needs.

All you have to do is listen carefully and pray for yourself and study your Bible. Arm yourself with the

Word of God and He will direct your path. Always keep in mind that Satan was once an angel in heaven who fell from glory because of his arrogance and he knows the word of God very well. So, therefore, he can manipulate it when he knows that you do not know the word nor study. You can't rely on the pastor to be the one to get you in the gates of heaven. He is just a man, and he makes mistakes, just as we all do.

You must know that your salvation is just that, YOURS! You study for yourself so that you will be able to discern the truth from a lie and a from b. Sometimes you put too much faith in the man and not enough faith in God. The Bible says, **"trust no man."** Therefore, your trust must be placed on the sure win, and that is in God. **"For God will never leave you nor forsake you."** Trust that God will guide you to the right teacher and the right steward.

Be aware of the ones that only teach prosperity and giving. You must be taught and guided by someone who will gently correct you when are wrong and sticks to what the scripture says and not condemn you to hell every time you sin. Yes, you are still going to sin when you become saved. Oh yes, I did! You are a human being housing a spirit being, ladies and gentlemen. The flesh is weak and even if you do not use your body to sin your mind can do it for you. What I mean you say, well the word of God says that, **"if you think it, then it is so."** Having a lustful eye is a sin.

Listen being saved does not give you an automatic off button that just turns off your nature or natural self. You must learn to train your body not to do certain things anymore, and it does not and will not happen overnight. It is a process that requires hard work. It is a moment by moment process, not a daily one because we go through so many changes that waiting to pray just once a day is not enough. You must practice being conscience of your spirit. Just as you are of your body. We learn to sit before crawling, and then we learned to walk before running. Well, that is the same concept with working on your spiritual relationship with God.

Again be mindful about making the choice to allow someone to speak in your life and over your life. This must be done carefully because words can either build a spirit or destroy one. You will be able to tell easily who is for you by listening to the words that they speak to you. Even the word of God says that, **"iron sharpens iron."**

« 18 » A VIRTUOUS WOMAN

ARE YOU A WOMAN like that which the Scripture has spoken of? Are we as children of God above reproach? Do you consider yourself a virtuous woman? If the answer to these questions are yes and you are with a man that you are not yet married to, does he consider you a virtuous woman? If the answer to this question is no, then is he looking for a virtuous woman? The point of this chapter is to open your eyes to the fact that the man that you are with may not be on the same page as you. You may have started out with a common goal but somewhere along the line went in two separate directions.

We as women of God must stop and take a look at who we are with and why we are with them. Then we must truthfully take a step to ensure that the person we are with really wants to be with us and for the right reasons.

A true man of God is also going to examine you and your motives for being with him. He will want to ensure that you are the virtuous woman that God has ordained him to be with. At the beginning of **"Proverb 31,"** you learn about what kind of woman a man should look for and whom they should allow in their lives. Then in **"Proverbs 12"** we are taught the rightful way to be as children of God. How do we as children of God see ourselves? Do we have the right perception of who we are in the kingdom? When we are among one another are we truthful and realistic about our expectations towards one another?

I know that there are times when we hold back out of fear of being judged and put down because of some of the choices that we have made in our lives. We as children of God can sometimes be hypocritical towards one another and very self-righteous. We fail to keep in mind that we all have sinned and fallen short of the glory of God. That we all have made errors, and none of us are perfect. This hinders us from moving forward and truly operating in the fullness of who God is. This keeps us guarded and closed off. I can say this because this is me. I often been misunderstood and inappropriately judged by those that I allow in my life. I thought that a virtuous woman would not have a problem being located by a man of God. I thought that being who I am would attract the man of God that was designed for me to me.

I thought being honest about my life, and the things that have unfortunately happened to me would bring about overstanding and compassion, not more hurt and pain. I had no idea that this virtuous woman would have to endure belittlement and ridicule because of my faith. I have cried many tears trying to figure out what is it about me that keeps me making the same judgments in error. I have wished many days that I had a solid foundation on this planet in place for me growing up and even now for that matter.

In the word of God, Solomon told his sons what to look for in a woman so that they would not waste valuable time on the wrong ones. He armed them with the proper information. On his death bed, Solomon told his sons also about being careful who they allowed in their homes, befriended, connected with, and to finds themselves a virtuous woman to marry. As women of God, we also need to be instructed as to the right character of man that we are to be given.

We must be taught how to overstand the God given man that was sent to us. We must know as virtuous women that we are not intend to be perfect and that the man of God that's sent to us is not perfect as well. We both must be realistic about our expectations of the other and ask the proper questions so that we can make the best possible choice for our lives. You must ask, is that person best suited for you? And if not, then you must ask yourself when do you end it?

There is no need in wasting valuable time on someone that you know is not the person for you. Remember time is the most precious resource we have, so use it wisely. Don't fall victim to the hype about, oh girl, what's the rush? You have plenty of time. You must also keep in mind that the man that

God sends to you is already complete. It is not your job to complete a man because you can't, that is only for God to do. This man of God must be complete by having an active relationship with God, and so are you.

When joined together you are made whole. Two joined together and made one. Meaning that your one is a whole not broken into fragmented pieces that can't be mended and expecting a miracle from a man or woman to put it back together. It is the power of God that heals us. That makes us whole. An outlet is still an outlet without the electrical item, but the outlet is made effective when the electrical item is pulled into it. We as human beings are powerful as individuals, but when connected to another human being we are even more powerful as children of God.

So the connection is a mighty powerful thing when done right. It is the man's goal to do whatever he has to do to make the marriage right. It must be two people working together for the common goal. In a union that God joins together, there must not be any separatism. It must always remain we and us because you are a team. You must make sure that God is the one who sent you that man because there are times when we choose and truly did not consult with God.

Overstand that what you ask for must line up with the will of God. Pray for God to show you and the other person to whom you think was sent to you. Also, make sure that you only submit to a man that is submitting to God. Make sure that you are with a man that is after God's own heart. He will not be perfect, but he will be the right one for you. He will also be God fearing, and he will also come with his own issues. You will have to ask yourself are you willing to take the risk? Can this man of God maintain his values and integrity?

This man must overstand that he must operate according to the will of God and that no one comes before his wife because she is the other half of him and he is to take care of her as such. We as women must also overstand that we are created to love and be loved. Therefore, nothing and I mean absolutely nothing should be allowed to interfere or stop you from experiencing love. Also, know that in love we must always forgive those who have hurt us because unforgiveness can hinder love.

You must make sure that the man that you allow in your life communicates with you on your level. The right communication skills are a must in any relationship. Lack of communication is the quickest way to end a marriage. Remember also that your job in the relationship as the wife is to be the help meet, not the crutch. You will know if you have taken on the job as the crutch when you start to feel robbed. Then you need to ask yourself, is the relationship draining you? Because it is not supposed to do that. It should be fulfilling, uplifting, and building you.

No one has the right to come along and mess up God's plan for you. The right person will guide you through. While the wrong person will slow you down, which will lead to a delayed purpose. Hindering the process of the right person to come along and if you have made the error of judgment and allowed the wrong person in don't beat yourself down about it. Don't allow that bad experience to stop you from allowing the love that you deserve to enter your life.

I know that it is easier said than done but you must find away. Yes, I am speaking from experience because I too have gone through the same thing but you can't allow Satan to win because God is love and love is vital to our survival as children of the Most High. That's why Satan tries to keep us from experiencing God in His fullness. Love is the key to unlocking any door.

I cry when I think of people who say that they don't need love or want it or call love a negative device or addiction. How dare you think that about God for He is love and worthy to be praised, wanted, and needed. If that be an addiction, then so be it. **"Hi, my name is Victoria, and I am addicted to God!"** I am not ashamed to admit that I need love, and I am not going to stop or hinder myself from experiencing it.

It is a shame that there are so many virtuous women out there who still have yet to receive the man of God that they deserve. A virtuous woman needs a good God fearing man that has himself together. A man who has an active relationship with God. A man who knows his place in the kingdom and a man who is ready to be the husband that God ordained him to be. A virtuous woman must know her role as well. She is to cultivate, nurture, and stretch her man of God. She must press him to be better and to excel and achieve greater heights. She is his encourager, confidant, and friend. She is his favor.

We as women of God must also overstand that it is not good to expose your weaknesses to a man before you truly know him well. Never bring up childhood traumas before the relationship has been established. Learn to live in the moment without putting too much energy in the past nor in the future because the present is all one has to operate in. I am not telling you to be dishonest. I am just simply saying, to ease your way into revealing your painful experiences, unless he asks you about it and even then reveal at your speed and when you are ready to do so. Don't discuss anything when you are feeling pressured.

When starting a new relationship, you must take the time to get to know as much about the person as you can before you commit yourself to him. Ask questions and a lot of them and check him out. It is okay to do these things. It is best to know up front than to deal with a disastrous situation later.

Be realistic when dealing with him and know that no matter what you do, you will never truly know everything about anyone. However, do your best to arm yourself with as much information as you can about that man of God.

Also, keep in mind again that he is not without flaws and neither are you. Do not judge him and do not make your decisions based on his talents or gifts but rather on the spirit of the man. As children of God, we must overstand that we have a purpose, a destiny, and assignments, and we must have a divine partner who can help us achieve those goals through togetherness, worship, prayer, praise, and love. Through God's direction. Think and pray before committing. Having God's direction placed upon you through prayer will enable you to lessen your mistakes.

We must at all times seek the balance of truth for a false balance is an abomination to God. Look deep within yourself and learn everything you can about you. Yes, you! Get to know the beauty of who you are and how to operate in your spiritualness.

A man wants a woman who takes care of herself in all areas of her life and as a woman, you should also want a man who does the same. If you do not have your divine partner yet, don't get discouraged. While waiting, take the time to better your relationship with God, and if you are not where you need to be as a virtuous woman of God, then this is the time to do what is required to be her.

A man of God will have character, and his character is not determined by how handsome his face is or by the car he drives. His character is shown in the way he is and the things that he does along with the words that he keeps. He must be a man of his word. Anyone can say something but do they do what they say. Is he loyal to you? Does he make you his priority? Does he show you, love?

A woman must look for who loves her with their actions and not just by the words that proceed out of his mouth. Simply put, do his actions line up with his words.

When a man truly loves you, there's no limits as to what he will do for you. He will be committed, respectful, caring, giving, and all the things that he should be to the gift that God has presented to him for he knows that you are his link to the limitless favor of the Most High. Don't be afraid to set standards for yourself, just be realistic about what you want.

Choosing the right person is very important to your future. Keep in mind that just because a man chooses you does not mean that you have to accept him. You have to make sure that you and him are compatible and have common interests.

Every time a person chooses the wrong person that diminishes what is inside of them. It takes a chunk off of the core of who you are. Being connected to the wrong person takes away from the spirit you. Especially if you are with an abusive person and remember abuse does not have to be physical. Abuse of any kind is never acceptable. If you are still unattached, you need to take a moment to ask yourself, why are you still alone? Why is a great woman of God having difficulties attracting the right man of God?

You need a plan, and most people are operating in a plot, and these two can't exist together. While you may have a plan for your life, the person that you are with may have a plot for your life, a scheme per say. Be careful! Watch out for people who prey upon you, instead of praying with you. You must be on one accord. Everybody has at some point in their lives been with the wrong person. The time has come to attract the right person. I know you are wondering. Well how do I do that? You know, in the beginning, Christ had to hand pick His twelve disciples out of many. With that being said you have to pray and ask God who the right person is for you. Always ask God when you are feeling good and on an upswing. Never ask Him when you are low and feeling down because doing so will allow doubt to sink in and lessen your ability to hear God's voice.

When you do decide that you have the right person take a good look at his life and if he is uncomfortable with the way things are in his life don't run nor become discourage because this is a good sign. Yes, you read it right. It is a good sign because a sign of being uncomfortable means that he is striving for excellence. Pushing to better himself and he has set goals that he has yet to reach. That is a man with a vision, a purpose, and a plan.

You need a man of God that can stand with you in your discomfort. One who will be there when you have nothing to offer him but you. A soldier ready and willing to do whatever he has to do for your betterment. He has to be a man seeking God. You need a man that will speak blessings over your life when things are against you. Who will uplift and encourage you even when you can't do it for yourself. A man who will add to you and not take from you. A man that builds you and not tears you down.

You must choose very carefully and remember that

no man is perfect and that your man of God has flaws, but the major things that he is supposed to have are all there, just with some minor kinks of course. Also, keep in mind that when the right man of God comes along, so does Johnny come lately. You know the one you thought was the one. The one who walked away with no reason. The one you prayed would come back. Well here he is, back after all that time and just when you and the true man of God have made your vow and commitment with one another.

Oh, baby please, don't fall for the trick of the enemy because that's exactly what that is. He only came back because he was sent by Satan to try to disrupt the will of God. The devil is a liar and will do anything he can to stop the plans of God over your union. You must be mindful of his devices because they can be easily missed. Satan doesn't like marriage because it is a covenant between man, woman, and God. Marriage in itself is a ministry. God wants you to be married and to be fruitful and to multiply.

However, the devices of the enemy are to ensure that you stay single, and if you do marry, he wants to ensure that you get a divorced. Listen, God said that, **"it is not good that man should be alone."** This is clearly stated in the word of God in **"Genesis 2."**

When God has placed the right man in your life, please remember to rejoice and be thankful for the blessing that God has so graciously given you. Your union is to be nurtured and cultivated so that it can grow stronger and more loving as each moment passes. Spend time together being loving and caring towards one another so that when disagreements come you have those times to keep you grounded. Never let the sun go down on your anger because by doing so you give a foothold to the enemy to come in and disrupt and even destroy your relationship.

Keep God in your relationship both as a couple and as children of the Most High. You must pray together daily and nightly. Proper communication, is the key to successfully managing any relationship. You must not shut down the lines of communication because silence is deadly in a marriage. Talk about it, let it all out but do so in a loving and respectful manner. It is the way in which we deliver some words that make them harsh and hurtful. Remember your tongue has the ability to help and harm.

« 19 » ATTRACTING A TRUE MAN OF GOD

THERE IS SOMETHING TO be said about a true man of God. He is a builder by nature, and I am not necessarily speaking of things. I am speaking of people. He is willed by God to lift others up, especially the favor that God has placed in his life. He knows his true place in the kingdom and is not puffed up or arrogant about it. He is however very sure of himself and humbled by the thought of God using him in His kingdom. He is a nurturer and a lover of the mission that God has placed him on. He knows that he is the protector of those that God has placed in his life.

He is not afraid to cry in front of a virtuous woman and relishes in the thought of showing her all sides of him for he is not ashamed of who God made him to be. He also acknowledges that he is a servant to the Most High God and knows with that knowledge comes the responsibility to be the best man that he can be. Even when he has made an error, he quickly does what is required to correct it. He is anointed to study you as his favor. That man will not do anything that would cause the plan of God to be delayed in your life because he knows that you and him are one and that whatever he does to himself he also does to you.

So while waiting on the divine man of God, you must increase your knowledge of self and overstand what it truly means to be a virtuous woman of God. To know that you are a gift to be treasured and what God's plan is for your life and that it is an honor to be a true servant of God. Preparations are to be made for the attack that is going to come against you and the man of God that is coming.

Oh yeah, Satan is going to attack because he knows that covenant with God is strong, and he doesn't want you to be fruitful. When your union creates the flow of God in your life to bring forth the next generation of God's anointed warriors, the enemy will not rest until such plans are derailed.

We as women of God must know that we must overstand that there is an attack on the anointed and Satan will send a man to you to block the purpose on your life and the divine husband that he has created for you. You are favor, and Satan wants to take that away from the anointed man of God that He has assigned to you. There will be obstacles thrown at you from every angle even sometimes from the man of God placed in your life because Satan knows how to use those closest to you to derail the plan of God on your life. That's why you must as a family stay prayed up. **"A family that prays together stays together."**

Your divine man of God will be strong and weak. He will need you to help him meet the goals, plans, and deeds that God has placed upon him. He will also need you to build him when he is down and to be strong in his weakness, and he will do the same for you. This man will pray for you without you asking and will build up his favor in her time of weakness as well. He will not be critical towards you but rather he will be uplifting and encouraging. He will be protective of you because he is aware that without you there is no him.

He seeks you in all areas of his life. He guides you towards him with gentleness and meekness. He is respectful of your anointing and does what is required to keep the peace in your household because he knows that Satan doesn't want the plan for God on your union to prosper.

Marriage is a sacred bond between man, woman, and God. There is no room for the enemy. So when you have filled everything that you are with the spirit of God, then, **"no weapon formed against you shall be able to prosper."** You will stand mighty and strong together in the name of God.

You must realize that you are for him, and he is for you. That you must spend quality time together studying, loving, growing, and living in the will of God as a couple. **"A house divided will not stand."** That is why God ordained unions. See, there is strength in numbers. The word of God says that, **"one can chase away a thousand while two can chase away ten**

thousand."

So in your time of waiting on your divine man of God, please don't give up. Know that God is preparing him for you and the proper cultivation is key to the proper union. The key word here is proper not perfect. However, you will never have to beg your man of God for anything because love just does. His thoughts of you will make sure that he looks for extra ways to bring joy to your life because he is aware of who you are and whose he is. It is imperative that you have a keen eye out for those that appear to be what they are not. Those that claim to be sent from God when actually they are Satan's spawn. This is where you studying and getting into God's presence will truly pay off.

Those times that you were alone and learning who you are and deepening your bond with God will help you to weed out the good from the bad, the fake from the real. Ladies always remember that a Bozo will always appear before your Boaz. Yes, there will be clowns in your future to deter you from the divine man that has been appointed to you. The enemy will use every trick in the book to steal you from the will of God. Just know that it is okay to say no and to have standards and to even change your mind if you feel that you have made a mistake. It is important to overstand that hurt people tend to hurt the people closest to them.

Take the time to truly get to know yourself and what makes you happy. Then open up your heart to receive the divine man of God sent to you. No one on this earth can heal you. That is a job for God. So do not expect your husband to heal all the wounds that were inflicted upon you before he came along. This healing should be placed upon the altar of God. Yes, your divine man of God can assist you in the process, but it is not his duty to take the blame for what others had done to you before he came along.

Remember, you must stay current in order to heal. Say to yourself when you become bitter and sad about your past that it is just that, your past. You are no longer there in whatever it was. Open your eyes and look around yourself and truly see where you are with a fresh pair of eyes. Take a deep breath and smell the beauty of your surroundings. I suggest that you even hug yourself, tight. It is imperative during those times that you speak out loud and say that you are safe. It is also imperative that at times like these you constantly remind yourself that you made it out of that trauma and that you survived.

Lift up your hands, throw your head back and thank God for His mercy. It is okay to remember, just try not to dwell in the memory. Look for things that have brought you great joy. Those joyous memories will quickly bring you out of the despair. Laugh as much as possible and do something childlike. Go to the circus, zoo, theme park and play. Bring back that childlike innocence will help in the healing process.

Now once you have begun the healing process, you will start to see yourself for whom you are deep within and then you will start to attract the people who will treat you with love and kindness. You will start to see things through brand new eyes. You will no longer accept the mistreatment that you use to, and you will adopt a brand new sense of awareness. You will be more in touch with the spirit you, and this will open up new doors for you in every realm.

During this time be aware of how you treat people. You do not want to start neglecting those new healthy people that have come into your life during your healing process. Keep those that are positive in your close circle. Being aware of those that are for you and against you is important to staying emotionally healthy. You need positive support and encouragement around you at all times because the challenges will still come and there will be moments when the memories will come like a flood, and you will need people that can uplift you in those times especially when you are not able to do so for yourself.

Do not be ashamed when these times arise, it is completely normal for a survivor of any trauma. Talk positively to yourself daily. **"I am more than a conqueror. I am loved, wanted, and desired. I am above and not beneath. The head and not the tale."** Keep speaking life into your situation and know that God has you covered, especially during your time of waiting.

I know that it is not easy to be alone because God even said that it is not good. So keep pressing toward the mark of healing and know that God is also preparing your divine husband for you. Never give in to the negative talk of others about giving up because of your age, social stigmas, or whatever. You must remain positive and steadfast about what God has told you and know that you do have a divine partner, and you are not meant to be alone because there is someone that God designed just for you. So hold your head up and get yourself in shape because there is plenty to do before your divine husband arrives.

Get into your word and learn what it means to be a virtuous woman and a wife to a truly anointed man of God. It is a must that you, a woman of God, know what it means to be submissive. Submission has nothing to do with weakness. It is the complete opposite. True submission requires a spiritual strength that not many have. It is about being completely secure and trusting of God in a way that allows Him to shine completely through you.

Your duty to that man of God is to be of service to him as he is of service to God. Knowing that submitting to him is in honor of whom God is in your life and that it is not because of weakness that you have this task, but it is rather due to strength. Strength is a must when you are with a man of God because his chosen path is not an easy one and he will need a strong woman of God to help him navigate through the daily crap that is thrown his way. He needs to know that you have his back not matter what comes his way.

You are his safe haven away from the problems of the world. When he comes to you, he must know that you can soothe whatever has come against him. That, there is comfort in your words, deeds, and actions. That you are his favor from God and the link to divine purpose. He will look at you with adoration and promise because he knows that God gifted you to him. It is something amazing when a man knows that the woman in his life is a gift from God. There are no limits as to what he will do for you because of this knowledge.

Your man of God will be a protector and a nurturer. He will make sure that you know that nothing will separate the two of you and that he will be there, as the head, just as God has required without hesitation.

Your man of God will notice things about you that no one else has because he will study you. His every thought will be towards how to be a better man in your presence. He will make it his job to know what it is that makes you, you. From the way you hold your head slightly to the left, to when your period is going to come on. He will be more in tuned with your body that he is with his own. Your natural scent will arouse him, just as when you enter a room, his body will instinctively gravitate to yours. This is what is meant by being of one flesh. It will flow so naturally that you won't have to think about it.

When you are meant to be together certain things just, are. It flows like water down a stream. Just please be aware that sometimes your flow will have to go over some rocks and rough terrain but during those times, remember that you are just where you need to be and with whom you need to be with.

Don't confuse your feelings with your faith because even when your man of God appears you will second guess it. Why? Simply because you have been waiting so long and you have been through so many failures and even considered giving up.

I know just how you are feeling because I too have been there and as I am writing to you I am still here, but I have faith that God is preparing my Boaz for me as I write this for you, and I will not allow my feelings of despair to stop my faith. I know that I am a virtuous woman in waiting and my Boaz is being prepped and primed for me. So I tell you the same things that I tell myself. I know what you are feeling, and I know that you too will come out of this as more than a conqueror.

Nothing on this earth can stop you, other than you! You are your worst enemy when it comes to faith and rejoicing in the promises that God has placed on your life. We as the body of Christ must learn that how we perceive ourselves is the key to the collective evolution that we need to transform our lives for the positive. If you trust in God, then the pain and you will come to pass. God has already ordained you for a time such as this. So get up, and start pressing past your pain, and doubt. You can do this. So hold on, the victory is near. You are not meant to be alone, and you won't be alone much longer.

Learn the lesson that God has given to you, so that you can gain the reward. Be whatever it is that you are seeking, and it will come to you. We must learn to attract that which we are praying for by becoming it. Okay, you want a loving, compassionate, giving, God-fearing husband. Then become a loving, compassionate, giving, God-fearing wife. Forget all of that crap, about opposites attract and think about the same game principles.

If you are playing "monopoly," then why do you have "sorry," pieces? The point being, you have to arm yourself with the same information that you are trying to attract to you. Learn and do research on everything that you can find out about the type of man that you are praying for. Study yourself and what makes you tick. Who are you? What are your likes and dislikes? What are the relationship deal breakers for you? If you don't know who you are and the answer to these questions, then how do you expect to attract someone who does.

Become confident in whom you are, whose you are, and what you want. Then put a plan in motion to become all that you can be for yourself. Work on your mental, physical, and spiritual self. These tools will arm you with the strength that you need to say no to what you don't want and hold on to those moments when it looks as if he is never going to come. Expect him at any moment, pray for him daily, and encourage him through your positive thoughts.

You must learn to do these things now so that they will become second nature when he arrives. It is very important that you know your role as a wife of a man of God. You are the one who stands in the gap for him spiritually. The word of God says that, **"you are to bruise the head of the enemy for your husband."**

Please don't take lightly your role in your Divine partner's life. It is imperative that you know what it is that you must do as his help meet. No one on this earth can help him the way that you can. He needs you! More than you will ever really know. Your role is an important one that should not be taken lightly. So during those times when the enemy comes in like a flood trying to get you to doubt your husband and the plan that God has placed over the bond that you share, don't fall for it. Hold you head up high and stomp your foot. There, you just did it, you bruised the head of the enemy.

« 20 » WHO HOLDS THE KEY

WHO HOLDS THE KEY to the chains that bind me? Bound by the thoughts that threaten to cripple all that God has ordained me to be. Who, I say who holds the key to the chains that bind me? Created free, and then captured by defeat, willing the freedom to come after me. Who holds the key to the chains that bind me? Stretching forth my hand, praying for the man that bound and gagged me, telling me sweet lies while singing cryptic lullabies. Who, I say, who holds the key that binds me? Eyes so rare, skin so soft, flair still there. But there's no depth to the eyes, shine to the skin, nor compassion to the flair. I look around and wonder how did I get there. There in a place filled with shamed, betrayal, disgrace, plastic smiles on everyone's face. Who holds the key to the chains that bind me? Hand to my heart, the other to my head wondering why I feel so empty, lost, and dead. Searching for the me I use to be. Wondering why I let these chains bind me? Broken from memories that flood my mind. Trying to stop the dam from breaking before I run out of time. Mauled, maimed, torn into tiny pieces wondering if I can mend what use to me, completeness. Who, I say who holds the key to the chains that bind me? Rocking myself the way a loving mother soothes her crying baby. Patting my own back and cheering myself on, looking for an outlet to escape from this raging storm. The clouds have thickened, the sun has gone, the darkness nears me as I try to hold on. Who holds the key to the chains that bind me? This storm is stronger than I could have ever imagined and I feel saddened when I look at the damage she has left behind. Catastrophe has caught up and bound me, crippling my feet, blocking my path, knocking me straight on my ass. Who, I say who holds the key that binds me?

I often think about what it is that I need to do to change the course of events that have occurred in my life. Yeah, I know what you are thinking. What if, just what if you could somehow alter the course of your downward spiral and come out of the storm victorious. I know that it is possible. See, what I have learned is that when we are in a negative slump in our lives, it is because we have created it with our thoughts. If you can change the pattern of your thinking process, then you can change the course of the negative forces in your life.

Just think about this for a moment. If a magnetic is only attracted to that which is similar, then so are you. When you start to have negative thoughts about yourself, you will attract that which you are thinking of. Such as, if you constantly tell yourself that you are going to fail, then you are. However, if you start to tell yourself that you are going to succeed, then you will.

Everything starts with a thought. This is where your battle begins, in the mind.

Research shows that when you are told negative things for so long, you begin to think them even when they aren't true. This, in turn, causes an internal battle. You struggle to hold onto that which you know is the truth based on the lies that have been embedded deep within you. I have learned during this course called my life that many things aren't always what they seem. You can be right there in the midst of whatever it is and still misinterpret the truth. Yes, we are human and flawed.

There's always three sides to every story. Yes, I said three. Your side, their side, and the only side that truly matter's and that would be God's side. We as human beings act and react to what we see around us. We are so off key to our spiritual side that we allow our negative emotions to control us. For example, when someone hurts us we what to hurt them back. Instead of going to God and asking Him what it is that just happen and why? Why is this person behaving in such a matter that is causing them to inflict pain upon me?

People who are in pain whether it is physical, mental, or emotional tend to inflict pain on others simply because they are in pain. No, it is not right nor fair, but it is so. The bad part about it is that sometimes they aren't even aware of what they are doing. Even when you try to bring the matter to their attention, they do not see it as you do. There are times, when you are trying to correct someone else's error, and you can cause yourself great harm because very few people what to be corrected, even when they know that they are wrong.

This area must be treaded upon carefully and always with prayer first. Ask God what is it that you need to say and to please govern your words so that the person who needs correcting can lovingly receive them. Sometimes after you hear from God, He has instructed you not to say anything because He will handle it for you. He knows what we need before we even need it. I have painfully learned that sometimes it is best not to say a word to anyone but God. I have often failed when I have tried to handle things myself and the damage still has not been repaired.

Your mouth can kill a person's spirit if used the wrong way and on the flip side of that, your mouth can bring life to a person when used the right way, as well. You can govern your words accordingly and change the course of a person's life without even knowing it. Be kind and loving when thinking of correcting someone and just because you can say it doesn't mean that you should. Our words have the ability to scar a person for life, and I have spoken of this often.

I would hope that by constantly saying it that someone would get it. Silence is not a sign of weakness, it is a sign of strength to remain quiet in the midst of thunder. I know that it is hurtful when someone you love is lashing out at you and saying hurtful things. I also know that it is easy for you to say hurtful things back but I pray that you would take a moment and process your relationship with God.

Now take a deep cleansing breath and silently pray and ask God to be your strength and to guard your words. Look at the person who is lashing out and think of the way God has forgiven us when we have wronged Him. Think of how God sent His only begotten son to this earth to die for atonement for our sins and Jesus did nothing wrong, yet He paid the price for our wrongdoing. Wow, is it worth arguing about now? Do you have to plead your case and show them just how wrong they are? Or are you going to say lovingly, God I thank you for loving me even when I didn't love myself? Are you going to examine yourself instead of examining the other person's behavior?

Yes, I know they did you wrong. Yes, I know that you are right. Yes, I know that it's not fair. Neither was it to the Lord, but He still endured to the end so that we could be saved. Was it easy for Him? No. Is it easy for us? No. Is it God's will? Yes. Someone has to show the unsaved what it is like to be the saved. We must hold ourselves to a higher standard because of whose we are. God wants us to walk in His glory and hold our heads up when all else seems to be failing.

He wants us to trust that He has us covered even when others have wronged us. Especially to those that have wronged us. We must learn to show love to the unloved and compassion to those who lack it. It is easy to love those that love us, but God wants us to show those who aren't aware of him what true love, compassion, and forgiveness is. He wants us as His children to walk with the holes that others have placed in us to be filled with his light so that it shines forth in the midst of our dark places so that others can see Him in us.

It is sad when I sit back and think of what it is that I have done to myself and others by not truly comprehending that which God has said to me. I have been filled with so much anger and hurt that I could not fully overstand what God was trying to show me. I would shut down in a way that left me void of overstanding of my purpose here on this Earth. Even as I sit here, I am in awe as to just how much I have truly missed because of my need to prove that I am not stupid. I have missed the mark yet again by not embracing who I truly am in Christ. For fear of being dehumanized. So what if the world sees me as such. It is God's approval that I am seeking not man's.

This pathway to my liberation has been paved with many mistakes, but it has also been paved with many victories such as this one. The moments like this one when I can see the errors of my ways and correct them if possible. However, if the possibility for correction is not deemed possible then, at least, I can say that I learned the lesson from it and prayerfully ask God for forgiveness and move on. No one on this earth truly knows the pain of another because we all process information differently.

We can as children of God sympathize with those who have been traumatized especially when we have had a similar experience. However, the full magnitude of their pain can only be felt and identified by the one who has unfortunately lived through it. It is those experiences, that have shaped and molded us for whatever good or even bad that we possess. I do not know why certain things happen and no matter how much I try to overstand, study, and even analyze it, there is still never a logical explanation for any of it.

We all know that good and bad exists and that they are opposites of one another. But what some of us fail to realize is that these two forces are always at odds with one another and that we must work at doing the right thing at all times because wrong is always in our presence, no matter how much we pray, fast, and study.

Evil or bad knows no boundaries and will stop at nothing to conquer and rule over good. But I am here to tell you that God is good and good will never bow down too bad. It is only the appearance that bad is winning that drives some people to fall prey to it. It is through trickery and deception that the enemy uses to gain control of our lives. He knows that the human side of us sees the negative before the positive based on our painful experiences. So he plays that to the letter and shows us how all the wrong that others are doing is allowing them to prosper. Those are all lies because that stuff, that evil gains, comes at a much higher price than what you have paid, no matter how horrible and painful it was or even still is.

See, we as God's children are heirs to His throne, and we will not have to suffer always, and our reward is far greater than anything evil can conjure up. So you just hold on and stand firm in the fact that God has you covered and that no matter what you have gone through or are going through, **"He will never leave you nor forsake you,"** and He has endured every painful moment you have had and are having right there with you. He is omnipresent and feels all for His children.

Keep speaking goodness over your life and the lives of those around you and know that no matter what someone else has done to you, it does not mean that you have the right to do it to someone else. Please do not condemn others because of what someone else has done. The next man is not that man. So work on being present and fair to the new people that are set to come into your life and most of all, know that there is a difference between being cautious and condemning.

There is absolutely nothing wrong with being careful. You are supposed to learn from your mistakes. You will be somewhat guarded that's a given, seeing all that you have gone through. However, do not allow your fear to keep you in bondage and trap you into that single minded thinking. You are not meant to be alone and yes, there is a God fearing man looking for a woman like you. Yes, you, flaws and all. So I say, hold your head up and start preparing for what God has developed just for you.

Rejoice and know that God is real and He has heard your cries. Everything that you went through and are going through is not in vain. It is for the greater good of the kingdom of God. For it is through the test that the teacher is silent, but His silence doesn't mean that he is not presently watching and working. It is during His silence that you must apply all that you have learned and trust in the fact that God has prepared you for what you are going through.

« 21 » HURRY UP AND WAIT

I HAVE LEARNED THAT it is through our greatest pain that we are preparing to receive our greatest blessings. When things are so bad that the pain chokes you is when God is about to show up and show out. Your setback is a set up for your greater comeback. Victory is right there awaiting your arrival. I know that it seems so far away but trust in the word of God when He says that, **"through all bad some good must come."** You must in your time of waiting stay positive and know that you are not waiting in vain. God will do what He said He will do.

It is a very difficult thing to be without good companionship and positive support when you are going through tough times.

We all need support and love. No one wants to be alone. God surely did not create us to be alone and the sooner you realize this the better off you will be, especially when you start to doubt that there is someone out there for you. I know firsthand that nothing compares to being loved and adored. We are created in pairs, and a child of God will not be totally fulfilled without being connected to the one that God designed for you. So please, don't stop hoping and trusting that your divine partner is on the way.

As I stated before you must use this time of waiting as preparation for the love of your life. Become all that you hope to have because in order to attract compassion you must also be it. Yes, I know that it sounds corny, but it is the truth. See working hard on becoming all that you lack will give you a greater sense of accomplishment when you do gain what you have been so graciously awaiting. Some would like to think that he will come when you least expect it, but I disagree. I know that he will come when you are the most expectant of it. It is okay to be expectant of love and life, along with all that it in tells.

You have to want this more than ever before, in order for it to come to fruition. See, you have to become so willing to do the work that is required to get what it is that you desire. You must become passionate about this. I have learned that passion drives you to do the things that you normally would allow fear to stop you from doing. It's okay to want this. You must keep telling yourself that.

It is vital that you trust that you can and will have all that God has promised that you will have. It is imperative that you overstand that no one and nothing can be allowed to interfere with God's plans for your life.

« 22 » ACKNOWLEDGE

THERE ARE TIMES WHEN you can do nothing but pray. There are also moments when you have done nothing wrong but still suffer because of the wrong doings of others. No it is not fair and no I do not overstand when this happens, but you can rest assured that the actions of other's can delay your purpose. I have learned this first hand. I often look at the events in my life and scream out loud at the injustice that I have encountered. However, I also have to know that just as we can be hindered because of someone else's incompetents, we can also be blessed because of some else's competence. Yes, **"the prayers of others availeth much."**

I praise God for those who have interceded on my behalf. Those who aren't even aware that they were praying for me. Just the thought of it moves my spirit because I know that I am not here because of just my prayers.

This is meant for all of you who can't take another

blow. To those of you who can't hear another no. Please hold on to the thought that someone out there is praying for you. They are asking God to move on behalf of the unknown who can't say a prayer for themselves.

God knows just how you feel right now and He knows what you need. He has not abandoned you. Regardless of what others say, God is still on the throne, and He is still with you. Don't allow His silence to mislead you into thinking that He is not present because he is omnipresent even in His silence. I know firsthand that dealing with the unexpected things in life can leave you dazed and confused. It is when the unexpected happens that God is silent.

When you are going through the roughest and toughest times ever, you will more than likely not hear from Him. Keep in mind that during His silence you must remember the scriptures that you have studied. It's okay to be afraid and angry. Just don't give up.

I've spoken before about forgiveness, and I will do it again. You must learn to forgive others as well as yourself. Yes, we as children of God must learn to forgive ourselves for whatever we feel that we have done to ourselves and others. Forgiveness heals the wounded and repairs the damaged. It brings you into alignment with the God in you. It cleanses the filthy layers that keeps us from connecting with our spirit being. Christ knows our burdens and sorrows because He bared those on the cross. There is nothing under the sun that God is not aware of.

On this day 12/12/2012, I started with prayer and hope. I prayed for what I always pray for, and I hoped that what I prayed for would manifest into the physical. I am trusting God for the impossible and have struggled with the hurt, pain, and disappointment that comes along with trusting in impossible things. But there is something deep within me that will not allow me to give up hoping.

I know where I come from, but I have yet to know where I am going. My hope is that I will make it to where God says that I am too go. I have no one on this earth that is for me, but me. I cry outwardly and inwardly for who I am to be and who I am now. I want so very badly to be her. The Victoria that God says that I am. I struggle to see her, to be her. I know that every day I get up with the expectation of being her just to fall short every time, but I will not give up because I can't. I on my worse days can hear my appointed angels cheering me on.

This day has brought with it, such great disappointment because I had such high hopes for it and for me and again I fell short but if I awaken tomorrow, I will get up again expecting and hoping that it will be the day that my dreams may come true. I know that this day is a great day of spiritual alignment and awakening, and I pray that all that I have asked of God will become apparent in this physical world in which I dwell in, so that my physical self will become better connected with my spiritual self.

I know in my heart that dreams do come true, and I know that God is real, and He does hear me. Just as I also know that, I am not hoping in vain. My time has come, and all that God has spoken into my life has finally shifted with this day and aligned itself to bring forth that which is mine.

I speak on this day of 12/12/2012 into existence every blessing that God has released from heaven for me. Every prayer that I have thought and spoken that has aligned with the will of God has now on this appointed day been released. I claim back everything that has been taken and stolen from me. I tear down every stronghold and replace all negativity with abundant blessings and overflow. I speak life over my family and everyone I come in contact with. I pray for those known and unknown, seen and unseen events and occurrences. I call forth my fleet of Warrior Angels and Guardian Angels to continue to do the job that they were set forth to do on my behalf. I ask that every question that I have asked of God that I have not clearly heard the answer, to be answered again in a manner for which I will not miss the answer at this moment. I thank you, God, for my prayers for they have already been answered, yes, in Mighty Name of The Most High God, I pray, Amen.

« 23 » DECISIONS

WHO IS IT THAT gets to decide what we do and how we do it? We as human beings would all like to think that it is, us. That each of us as individuals get to, collectively decide what it is that we want and need to do, right? Well, what if I told you that there are other forces at bay that influence what otherwise would have been your true decision making. The process of, making decisions are more than likely based on the things that are going on around you at the time.

We as human beings tend to gravitate to that which is easiest or less complex especially in what I consider to be the microwave era. Oh yes, I have been guilty of this as well. The simple things are the easiest to control when it comes to the masses. Whether it be the subliminal messages given through the television, radio, or the internet. It is safe to say that all around us are portals of suggestion. Even the people we love try to do it as well. Being even bold enough to say it right out as such: **"I am simply suggesting that you**

do this." Really? There are those of us who catch it and others who simply do not.

Decision making is a very powerful tool because it is through the choices that we make that can either lead to greater joy or sorrow and even life and death or the quality thereof. I have looked back over my life and have both laughed and cried when I realized that some of the decisions that I made were based on someone else's ideas. Then, therefore, my decision actually in retrospect was their decision made for me. Yes, when someone has the ability to manipulate you into thinking their way or doing their thing then that's control over you. No matter how slight it is, manipulation is a very power weapon and being able to manipulate a person's decisions is, even more, powerful.

It reminds me of the Jim Crow crap which when looked at was utter madness and truth. To pit a set of people against one and another and allow them to totally destroy themselves without putting a finger on them is for lack of a better word sheer genius. See if those same people would simply study themselves and learn what their own weakness' are and change them thus becoming strong then who would those same people be? The battlefield is not land; it is the mind. If you can change your mind, then you can change your circumstances.

I don't care what the statistics say because those are based on false doctrines anyway. You can't keep allowing the biases of others to dictate nor control who you are. No matter what your circumstances are, you can come out if you truly want to. You must first realize that you are being influenced and manipulated by someone else. Manipulation is a tool used to control an individual. Manipulators are clever at their craft because they have taken a lifetime to cultivate their skills.

Webster defines manipulation as: **"To treat or operate with or as if with the hands or by mechanical means, especially in a skillful manner. To manage or utilize skillfully. To control or play upon by artful, unfair, or insidious means especially to one's own advantage. To change by artful or unfair means so as to serve one's purpose."**

The only goal in the mind of a manipulator is to get what they want by any means necessary. It does not matter if you are hurt in the process. They will lie, cheat, steal, and even kill to get what they want. They are selfish. When dealing with a manipulator, you must always be aware that you are being misused. Even when it doesn't appear to be the case. They are masters at seduction and sweet with their tongue. They will even make you think that everything that is happening was your idea.

"You must be as wise as a serpent when dealing with them and as humble as a dove." The reason being is because a master manipulator has the ability to become very dangerous. So when you find out that you are in the midst of one, you must always be on your toes. Never let them know that you are aware that you know who and what they are. Plan your escape as quickly as possible. Your goal is to beat them at their own game. These people use your fears to control you. They study you.

So it is in your best interest to study those that you allow in your life as well because it is beneficial to you in every area. Even the bible says to, **"study to show thyself approved."** I take that literally in every area of my life. See people only allow you to see certain facets of who they are and it is up to you to find out the rest. Some would say that this is wrong, but I am inclined to disagree based on the experiences that I have had in my life. Lord knows as I look back in time I often find myself wondering why I did not use the skills that I use now to assess the people around me. You can learn a lot about a person just by looking and listening to them speak.

You don't have to ask certain questions because I have learned that most people tell you more important and personal stuff when they think you are no interested in the information. So when allowing someone into your life get to know them by being silent. Listen intently to what they are saying and resist the temptation to talk continuously about yourself. To truly learn about an individual, you must look, listen, and analyze the very essence of who they are.

It is okay to know. You have a right to know whom you have in your life. Never allow someone to tell you what you can and can't do or say or feel. This is, in fact, your human right. Don't back down from what you know is what's right for you. You have to stand firm in your truth about you and your rights because if you don't, then who will? It is important to your survival to do so.

« 24 » PREPARATION

THERE IS NOTHING LIKE being readily available for the blessings of the Most High God. Preparation is key when you start allowing God to be whatever you need him to be for you. I have learned the hard way about asking God to give me something instead of speaking whatever it is into existence by allowing God to be who he is in my life. I have tried to overstand what it is that I need to do in this lifetime to get me where I need to be, just to fail repeatedly. I have determined that my lack of proper preparation has led me again to another failure. I am hardest on me. I examine myself daily, and I am not pleased with what I have found.

It is through my watchful eye that I have determined that I am more than deeply hurt by the things that have plagued my life. I am hurt to the very core of whom I thought I was. I walk around every day in this state of longing to be overstood. I am saddened to the point of agony. The closer I think that I am getting to God the further I am from Him. I have studied books and people only to determine that I do not belong here, and I am failing miserably at the assignment in which God has so graciously given me. I have failed to prepare fully for the task at hand. Foiled at Gods master plan.

I looked back over my life and realized that I have made some horrible mistakes and refuse to look at the good in which I have done because for me the good doesn't matter when you have done just as much bad. I have failed to love in the appropriate ways. I have failed to allow God to operate fully in my life, and even now I am failing. I am failing to overstand a system that allows children to be raped and do nothing, where men are abusers and blame the abused, where the pain is so deep that it penetrates the soul, where people walk around with no marrow to their bones.

I am failing to comprehend why the harder I press the less I am moved and why everything I do right is turned into a wrong and even why I have no peace in this place I call home. No one truly knows me or even wants to because they are so keen on making me into whom they say I should be. I grow even more tired as the minute's passed, wanting to revert to the old me and tell them all to kiss my, you know. Oh, but that wouldn't be, Christ like, you know. I am so sick of those who walk around thinking that just because you try to operate in the will of God that, that somehow makes them exempt from being accountable for their own actions.

Saying dumb crap like; oh, you should be the bigger

person no matter what the other person does to you, just take it and give it to God. Let me get this straight, just because I am a child of God that makes me devoid of feelings and a dumping ground for other people's bullcrap. I am an angry woman who relishes in God, who still operates in love, and who knows that I have a greater purpose than this mundane life that I am existing in. I know that somewhere deep within me I have a holy gift, but it is embedded so deep down in my soul that at times it seems unreachable.

I press and pull trying to reach that gift just to come up short every time. I miss the mark and then wonder why. I look around and see that I am not allowed to be me. I am a recluse, a hermit, a socially inadequate being who is misunderstood by all who come in my path. On a quest to attract someone like me only to realize that the quest I'm on is to find me. I am lost, searching to uncover the very essence of who I am and why did God leave me here to suffer amongst a people who hate the very fiber of my being, me.

I am a Nomad, who doesn't belong here. An outcast among those that supposed to love me but instead bind me with their hatred and bigotry. I have worked tirelessly to break the chains that bind me. Shackled by memories of betrayal, abuse, loss, and defeat. Only to have my inalienable right stripped from me. You know the one that's in the U.S. Constitution that states; **"I have the right to pursue happiness."** To pursue but not obtain, yeah, I know the name of this word game.

I am so tired of the pursuit just to never obtain,

chasing after something that was to be mine anyway. So I made up my mind to stop the chase and allow it to gravitate to me only to again come up short on my goals and dreams.

"So in this pursuit of happiness," this chasing down of dreams where did I go in the midst of this thing. Broken, shattered, cracked, marred, scarred, are labels that I have placed upon me as a way to remind myself of what I no longer want to be. I have decided to stop running from and to turn around and run to that little girl that nobody loved.

Yes, I have failed to prepare for this chase, and I am running last in this race, but I was told by The Most High God, that I have a trump card and that it's an ace. So yeah, I may be last, but I am going to finish this class and turn this around and make sure that my tail becomes the head before this life I have is over, before I am dead.

It is through self-examination that we find out who we are and during this process we also learn who others are in our lives. See, the clearer you see yourself you can then better see others. It is the clear vision that drives you to want to do better and be better than you were before. I often quote Shakespeare's, **"to thine own self-be true."** For if you are not true to you then how on God's earth are you going to be true to anyone else.

I have learned some very powerful lessons in this life and during this learning process that I am still in I can only say that I am tired of the madness. I know that there are challenges to life and that the unexpected does happen, and there is no way that you can brace yourself for some of the things to come about. However, prayer is a comforter, and it can be the joy that you need as well.

I have found that there are times when people lose sight of what is important and become selfish in their pursuit to happiness that no one else's feelings matter. When truth be told, that is the absolute wrong way to be when trying to excel in any area. We must at all times stay in tuned to whose we are and with that being said overstand that in the knowing must come a revelation. That we are still human, and it is okay to be tired sometimes, and it is okay to say, no.

We must acknowledge the fact that we aren't the true and living God and that we can't save those who do not want to be saved. Nothing in this life can stop you from being who God says you are, but you. You are the one that must keep that in mind and know that everyone will not be your cheerleader. Know that there will be times when you will feel depleted, and you will want to give up but with all those feelings, know that you can't give up because God won't let you.

You are destined for greatness as well as I am. We must learn to be comforters to one another for this road of salvation gets hard sometimes. We must also remember that nothing in this life is worth losing your relationship with God nor your relationship with self. You must at all times keep in mind that you are in a relationship with you. You must love you and nurture yourself. Yes, I know that it gets hard sometimes to do that, but you must keep trying because at the end of every day you are always with you. Full joy that and know that it is not a bad thing to have some alone time but also know that there are times when being alone is not a good thing. It is called balance, and we all must come to a point where we are operating in it.

As I continue the journey, I have decided to use some key principles that have been adapted by the Kwanzaa Celebration.

Kwanzaa is a week-long celebration held in the United States and also celebrated in the Western African Diaspora in other nations of the Americas. The celebration honors African heritage in African-American culture and is observed from December 26 to January 1, culminating in a feast and gift-giving.
Kwanzaa has seven core principles (Nguzo Saba): Unity, self-determination, collective work and responsibility, cooperative economics, purpose, creativity, and faith. It was created by Maulana Karenga, and was first celebrated in 1966–67. Kwanzaa celebrates what its founder called the seven principles of Kwanzaa, or Nguzo Saba (originally Nguzu Saba—the seven principles of African Heritage), which Karenga said "is a communitarian African philosophy," consisting of what Karenga called "the best of African thought and practice in constant exchange with the world." These seven principles comprise *Kawaida, a Swahili term for tradition and

reason. Each of the seven days of Kwanzaa is dedicated to one of the following principles, as follows:

1. **Umoja (Unity):** To strive for and to maintain unity in the family, community, nation, and race.
2. **Kujichagulia (Self-Determination):** To define ourselves, name ourselves, create for ourselves, and speak for ourselves.
3. **Ujima (Collective Work and Responsibility):** To build and maintain our community together and make our brothers' and sisters' problems our problems, and to solve them together.
4. **Ujamaa (Cooperative Economics):** To build and maintain our own stores, shops, and other businesses and to profit from them together.
5. **Nia (Purpose):** To make our collective vocation the building and developing of our community in order to restore our people to their traditional greatness.
6. **Kuumba (Creativity):** To do always as much as we can, in the way we can, in order to leave our community more beautiful and beneficial than we inherited it.
7. **Imani (Faith):** To believe with all our hearts in God, our people, our parents, our teachers, our leaders, and the righteousness and victory of our struggle.

Kwanzaa symbols include a decorative mat on which other symbols are placed, corn and other crops, a candle holder with seven candles, called

a kinara, a communal cup for pouring libations, gifts, a poster of the seven principles, and a black, red, and green flag. The symbols were designed to convey the seven principles.

This is a background on Kwanzaa for those of you who aren't familiar with Kwanzaa, and it's practices. I have decided to use these seven principles in certain areas of my life. However instead of using the seven principles for seven days I decided to use one principle a week. My first week starts off with **Umoja (Unity)** which means to strive for and to maintain unity in the family, community, nation, and race.

You would think that unity is a given when you are operating on this earth but it is not. We as a people are so divided that it has caused many generations of separation. I know that there are times when you just can't unite with some people because they are on a different path as you. However, as a whole, we must stop and take a closer look as to why we are divided and stop making excuses for it and take the necessary steps to do what is required to change this. It starts one household at a time. One phone call at a time. We each hold a power within us to change things no matter how small they may appear to be.

Showing one another love in a time when some think that love is not needed. We all no matter the spectrum need someone to love us and in order to operate in love, we must have unity. Being on one accord with someone.

We as human beings are built on the foundation of

love, and, therefore, we must operate in it and when we make a choice to go against who we are and whose we are then we disrupt the very nature of why we are here on this planet we call earth.

No one can fully function in the will of God without love. Love is the very essence of who God is, and He created you in His image and likeness, so with that being said, how can you being His creation operate in the life that He has loaned you without the love that you were created in? Unity and love go hand in hand because when you are united in God, then you are operating in His will. The key word here is God. I am not speaking of any demonic forces that be. This here is about the holiness that flows from the foundation of God and His children. About the balance that is needed by His children in order to gain back what we as a people once had, one person at a time.

I am not trying to discourage anyone but getting you to look at the grand scheme of things but to somehow empower you by showing you that it, "meaning this unit, can occur one household at a time." We are all somehow responsible for who we are as a unit because our souls are linked by the Most High God. We have to start somewhere, and it needs to be started when things are good and not when you see a tragedy happen to someone else that makes you angry enough to press out of the norm.

It shouldn't have to take an injustice for us to become unified. This unification should be automatic and a normal occurrence. We must stop giving our power as a people to other cultures because we fear stepping into the true oneness of who we are.

We as a people sit back and blame others for our predicament when the truth of the matter is, it is us. We are the ones who keeps us bound by not rising as a people. We can no longer blame anyone else for our lack of unity nor for the problems that plague us as a people. For it is us who should step back and examine us as a whole or a unit. **"We the people hold these truths to be self-evident that all people are created equal."** So with that being said, God, Himself has created us equally, but it is up to us, as a whole, to remain in the equal standing.

Equality is something that we as a people must demand when we feel that we are being treated unfair or unjust and not necessarily when there is violence or tragedy. When we bind together as a people through prayer, we become unstoppable. It is through prayer that we conquer our enemies because we are allowing the God that we serve the opportunity to be the **"shield and buckler"** for us as a people. We can no longer keep operating in the dormant stage of our spirituality, and we can no longer keep thinking that the prayers of our ancestors are going to keep carrying us.

We must begin to bond together and pray for those that are still here on this planet earth and also for those that are set to come long after our fleshly bodies are gone. No one can decide who we are to be to one another unless we allow them to do so and in a sense we have been doing just that. When does this madness stop?

Kujichagulia (Self-Determination): To define ourselves, name ourselves, create for ourselves, and speak for ourselves.

The time has come for us to rise up as a people and do that which we were called and chosen to do and that is to be leaders. The Kings and Queens that we rightfully are, but how do we as a people do that when we as a whole are afraid to speak for ourselves let alone, God forbid, someone else.

We have forgotten our names and who we are as a people. Oh, but this is a simple task that can be completed immediately by affirmation. We have the power and are afraid to use it so we stay stuck in a time warp hoping for someone else to come along and raise us up as a people, so that we can shout we have overcome, when what we really have done is coward down.

True overcoming means that you rise up, even if at first, you rise up alone. One person at a time, until you become a whole unit pressing forward for the greater good of the people. Who are we? Whose are we? What is your name? What have you created? What are you talking about? We must first individually, answer these questions for ourselves before we can move forward and teach someone else.

Who are we that we can't see past this mass hysteria? That we as a unit can't see the truth buried deep beneath the bed of lies? Why are we afraid to remove the tin from over these snakes? Why do we as a unit keep allowing deception to be fed to us for breakfast, lunch, and dinner? How do we move past our pettiness and start operating as a whole?

The uprising begins when we start teaching the word of the Most High God in its entirety and stop making excuses as to why we stay bound and work to put in place the active solution to this growing problem. We have the keys to breaking these mental chains that still bind us. We hold the truth that can make us free. We have the powers given to us by the Most High God to stop the senseless killings in our communities. We are the change that we seek. Everything that we have been searching for is already within us, but it is up to us to pull that which is within, out.

The truth wants to burst free, but it is up to us to allow that which is bound the freedom to be released. Even the word of God requires us to, "speak those things that are not as thou they were." We individually and together have the power to call forth what we need in this lifetime. Our voices and words hold power, however, that power can't be utilized until we give birth to it. I speak love, unity, peace, and abundance of knowing over all of us collectively. **"Selah."**

Ujima (Collective Work and Responsibility): To build and maintain our community together and make our brothers' and sisters' problems our problems, and to solve them together.

Everything that we are and can be as a people is linked to us as a whole. Yes, we have some power separately but just think of how much more powerful we can be as a whole body operating on one accord.

The word of God says that, **"one can chase away a thousand, and two can chase away ten-thousand."** Oh my God, just think if we as a people, would step into our chosen path and operate in the fullness of who we are meant to be just how many demons we as a people, can chase away.

Can you image one million of us praying together at one time in total harmony with the Most High God, how much we can accomplish in His Holy Name as a whole? We hold the keys to our collective work, and it is our responsibility to fix what we as a people have messed up. It is all of our duty to band together and work this out so that it will be beneficial to future generations to come. We as a body must pave the way for those that are to come behind us who will become those that are set to lead the people as God has ordained from the very beginning.

We must teach the youth the truth of our heritage and ancestry. Yes, all of it. The good, the bad, and the ugly and we must make sure that we do not place blame on others, for why we are the way that we are, as a whole or separately. Accountability is one of the first steps to healing.

Each one of us must be held accountable for what we have brought to the table of despair. Knowing that in this acknowledgment that freedom is dispersed. Now that we have held ourselves accountable, now we must work on a doable solution to that which was created out of fear and separatism. We can do this, and we must do this because if we don't band together and operate in the fullness, thereof, we will remain in bondage, as the damned will remain in control.

There is and have always been a solution before every problem is even presented. So, therefore, we must find that solution that best fits this problem and then effectively put the solution to work for the betterment of our people. I have found the solution to be the Almighty El Shaddai. He is and has always been the forefront to all that we are and hope to be. Without Him as our guide, we will not make it to the promise land.

No one can truly think for another human being when it comes to faith and spirituality. It is and has always been our right as able body people to think for ourselves. God has given each of us the capabilities to think for ourselves. I say that because there are times when we allow others to implant thoughts of what we should or shouldn't do. We have been given a mindset by God, and there are certain things that God allows us to meditate upon with this mindset. So, therefore, we must govern our mindset accordingly.

In the midst of the storm, there are times when you just have to be still and know that God has you covered. To bask in the knowing of protection from the Lord when all else fails. When the enemy tries to come in like a flood and destroy everything that God has been building in your life. But I say unto you just hold on and remain firm to that which you know to be the truth of the Most High God.

Allow nothing to deter you from the path in which God has placed you on because you do have a choice in the matter. There is always hope. In this struggle, you will face your greatest adversary, and that adversary is you. Once you learn to conquer that which hinders you from within, then you will be unstoppable. When we have been hurt, abused, and damaged so to speak, we become our hindrances and we must learn to stop the cycle of destruction that we place upon ourselves. No one can stop you from being who you are unless you allow them to. Nothing in this world is more painful than knowing that you have failed because of you. To be rejected because of someone else is one thing, but to be rejected from self is something totally different.

In learning and researching the principles of Kwanzaa, I learned that there is nothing more powerful than the self-determination in the face of adversity. If you are determined to succeed and move past where you are, then you can conquer anything. If you can find a network of people who are where you are going and latch onto them, you can see your way past where you are and be better able to come out of it.

You have to surround yourself with those that are where you need to be and step away from those that are where you are especially if that is where you don't need to be. We must learn that during the time of healing you must separate yourself from those that try to demean, belittle, and put you down. That is the last thing on this earth that you need at any time in your life, not just when you are in pain.

Love again is not painful, and it does not belittle, demean, nor put you down. Love is powerfully helpful, and it never destroys or takes away from. Love builds and adds to who you are and creates an atmosphere that will allow you to flourish and grow for the better. Love assists you in the area in which you need it and does not put unhealthy demands on you. You must have a firm foundation built upon love in order to survive in this world because no one can make it here on this earth alone.

Yes, God is that foundation that we must build upon and then we must pray for God to place His people in our lives to help cultivate us. A God-fearing community of people who can and will assist you with the path that God has so graciously chosen for you. This walk is not an easy one, and it is surely one that can't be taken alone.

Ujamaa (Cooperative Economics): To build and maintain our own stores, shops, and other businesses and to profit from them together.

It is imperative that we as a community pull together and do what is required from a business and economic standpoint in order to further our freedoms as an independent community collectively. We must teach our children the value of ownership. For without ownership we are still nothing more than modern day slaves, working to acquire wealth and riches for someone else.

We must learn to push our fears aside and step outside of our boundaries so that we can grow in the manner in which we should as a body of people. Banding together is the only way that we can reach those goals that were set for us by our forefathers. We are not meant to be in bondage whether that bondage, be in the mind or body. We must learn the value of ownership and stop settling for the scraps that others throw our way. We must as a people, teach one another the knowledge that was acquired, that allowed us to make it past that poverty mark, where we were able to pull up and offer assistance to someone else. As the scripture says, **"give a man a fish, feed him for a day; teach a man to fish and feed him for a lifetime."**

It is not okay that we considered it common, to have nothing to show for the hundreds of years of servitude to another body of people, who could still care less for us. The forty acres and a mule was just a fathom used to fool an already foolish set of people into thinking that they were going to get something that their forefathers were rightfully entitled too. For those of you who aren't aware of what forty acres and a mule is, let me give you a quick rundown on it as the historians would tell it to you.

40 acres and a mule refers to the short-lived policy, **during the last stages of the American Civil War during 1865, of providing arable land to black former slaves. Who had become free as a result of the advance of the Union armies into the territory previously controlled by the Confederacy,**

particularly after Major General William Tecumseh Sherman's "March to the Sea." General Sherman's Special Field Orders, No. 15, [1] issued on January 16, 1865, provided for the land, while some of its beneficiaries also received mules from the Army, for use in plowing. [2] Such plots were colloquially known as "Blackacres," which may have a basis for their origin in contract law.

The Special Field Orders issued by Sherman were never intended to represent an official policy of the United States government with regards to all former slaves and were issued "throughout the campaign to assure the harmony of action in the area of operations."[3] Sherman's orders specifically allocated "the islands from Charleston, south, the abandoned rice fields along the rivers for thirty miles back from the sea, and the country bordering the St. Johns River, Florida." Brigadier General Rufus Saxton, an abolitionist from Massachusetts, was appointed by Sherman to oversee the settling of the freed slaves. [4] By June 1865, about 10,000[citation needed] freed slaves were settled on 400,000 acres (160,000 ha) in Georgia and South Carolina.

After the assassination of President Abraham Lincoln, his successor, Andrew Johnson revoked Sherman's Orders and returned the land to its previous white owners. Because of this, the phrase "40 acres and a mule" has come to represent the failure of Reconstruction policies in restoring to African Americans the fruits of their labor. In testimony before Congress in 1871,

"forty acres and a mule" was attributed [by whom?] to be a promise made to African Americans by President Abraham Lincoln before he was killed.

Now that you have had your brief on 40 acres and a mule, lets get back to the topic at hand.

We have a select group of people who would rather kill than to release what is rightfully ours. So now we are at a point where most of us have given up on the dreams that we have because of the difficulties that we have faced and are facing today. However, I must say that we as a people can't go back. But we can move forward and operate in the now and build a better today for the generation of tomorrow, by building on the foundation that God has laid out before us, by banning together and opening up the mom and pop stores, and by learning what ownership is and teaching it to others.

We can start more business's and keep them in operation by shopping with one another and trading with one another. Bring back the days of co-oping. Just as our forefathers worked to build this country so that others would benefit from it. We can work to build and benefit for ourselves. Think about this. We as a body of people in the past, with nothing, worked as slaves and built this country and received nothing. So why can't we use the same work ethics and build a better place in the country for ourselves?

Once we start controlling some of the money

following into this country, we can gain some independence as a body of people. See, it is the money that makes lasting change in this country.

If you build your own stores, hire your own, teach your own, create your own, then you become unstoppable. Right now we are interdependent on the very people, who had us as a people, shackled and chained, literally. Oh yes, we are still slaves. Bound and gagged to a set of people who allow us to think that we have a voice when in all actuality they are telling you what to think and say and you are too dumb to even realize it.

Oh yes, see you buy their products because they tell you it's the best, when in all actuality they don't even buy their own products. You want whatever you see on their networks because you think that it is the best when you are really being; **"hoodwinked, bamboozled, lead astray, and run amuck"** as the late Malcolm X would say.

Someone has to be held accountable for what is happening to us, and the blame lies with us. Yes, us. When you would rather run out and buy a $150.00 pair of sneakers, gym shoes, tennis shoes: whatever the name is today, than to buy books or educational programs for your children, you are a fool. Yes, I said it. You bragging about the latest shoe on your foot but you have no knowledge of the world you live in nor where the very shoe that you are wearing came from. The sad part is that the very shoe you spent that much own is not even worth the price you paid for it and no one in your ethnic group even works at the factory that makes them, but you have made the creators of the product rich.

We as a people, have to stop being foolish. When you change your spending habit's, you change your life. Oh and don't get me started on the wasteful spending on fast food. The point that I am making is that we have some power, and it is not being utilized properly.

Nia is our next step in Kwanzaa. Nia (Purpose): To make our collective vocation the building and developing of our community in order to restore our people to their traditional greatness.

This really needs no more clarification than what I have already written earlier but for the sake of argument, I will reiterate. We as a people must study who we are as a body. We are the descendants of Kings and Queens from the shores of Africa. The blood of royalty flows through our veins. We must as a people get back to who we are as a body. We are no longer bound physically, but the mental bondage that we carry is weighing us down to the point where we are literally none functioning as a whole.

There is no other force of bondage other than us. Yes, us! We are the ones that hold us back. Therefore, we are the ones that have to set us free. The physical chains that once held our bodies are now holding our minds because we have made the choice to allow it. We as a body are mentally bound by labels, titles, and names. We as a whole own nothing but get mad at the fact that other's do. You would rather buy trinkets than to save your money for something that's really of value.

You have a whole bunch of nothing pretending like it's something. When you do obtain something, it goes quicker than it took you to gather it. Nothing is put away for a rainy day. You squander every dollar you get and wonder why you can't get ahead. During tax season, most of the working poor obtain a substantial amount of money, and before it even touches their wallet or purses, it is already spent on things that hold no value and that are not even needed. No bills are paid, and it is looked at as a go get it or party mentality.

It is a fact that within days of obtaining this tax refund the person is broke but as they would put it, fly. It is a sad and sickening concept that an opportunity to get ahead has been placed in their hands, and they squander it. Yes, I know that you can do whatever you want with your money. It is clearly your choice. However, there are other options out there, and if you are going to get out of the hole, you must first learn to take these opportunities and learn to save or invest in something that will allow your capital to grow.

We as a body must learn how to create financial independence for ourselves, and it can be done just by using some very simple principles. One very important thing you can do is only buy what you need. Necessity is the key to survival. Yes, I know we have conditioned ourselves to get what we want all the time but in order to break the chains that bind us financially, we must learn to budget our money. It is not as hard as we think is it. It is all about education.

Learning the proper information and then using that information to better yourself and then teaching that to others so that they too can prosper from it as well. It's the old adage; **"each one teach one."**

We must learn to incorporate education in every facet of our lives in order to excel in this game called life. There are many ways to gain that which is required to make it in this world. You can allow your needs to be what is wanted as well. We as a whole must learn to be truly thankful for our needs being met, and if those needs aren't met then, we must learn the tools that are required to get those needs met.

You do not have to go to college in order to acquire knowledge. You can do that within the confines of your own home. Utilize the internet and if you do not have access to that, then go to your local library and check out books on whatever topic that you are interested in learning. Even the bible says to, "study to show thyself approved."

We must dig deep within ourselves and realized that the bondage in which we operate in as a whole is vastly due because of us. Yes, we are our problem because we do not take responsibility for that which we have allowed to happen as a whole. Being continually bound in a place that offers so many hidden opportunities is a shame. Yes, there are things out there that we can obtain to make things better for us but without the knowledge that is needed, bondage is a given. Knowledge is power and learning from our past mistakes is a positive step to ensuring that our present is better. We must know where we as a people have been in order to know where we as a people are. The hope is in the changing of the now.

You can't have a better future if you are not utilizing the present that you are operating in. What can we do as a people today to help ensure that we live better lives tomorrow? That question is prevalent because many do not stop and take a look at today because they are so busy just existing instead of truly living. The sad part about this is that we as a whole will continue to use excuses as to why we are not operating in the fullness thereof. Until we rise up in the chosen path that The Almighty God has set before us.

We all have to get back to who we once were. The true Kings and Queens of Zion. We are the descendants of David. The true heirs to the throne of the Most High God. The Great I Am. I thank you, Lord, **"for never leaving me nor forsaking me."** It is through knowing whom we are and whose we are that we can rise up and be who and what we are chosen to be. We must acknowledge who we are as a people and walk in that. There is honor in knowing from whence you came and then taking that knowledge and walking in that purpose. You have to learn about yourself, and you do that by learning about your past and using that knowledge to function in your present and then therefore taking that and preparing for your future. Yes, it is just that simple. We as a people make it complicated when it actually is not.

Teaching ourselves is a must to rising up from the dung that we have placed ourselves in. Study the unknown heroes of the past. Those that fought and died so that you and I would have rights that most of us take for granted. Like the right to vote, read a book, speak the truth. Yes, those things that we as a human being are to have had in the beginning. Yes, we as a people were stolen and brought to this country against our will but now that hundreds of years have passed, what have you done with the freedoms that have been offered to you? Have you remained in a state of bondage? Are you still using excuses as to why you have not overcome? What will it take for you, yes you? To rise up out of the dung, that you have been so comfortably rolling in. It is easy to sit, and talk about change. However, real change comes when you are get up off of your butt and do something about it. There has to be some action with the talk. We must be a body of doers and not just sayers.

It starts right here and right now. There is a multitude of information out there to be learned and then taught. Starting with learning, you. Who are you? What are you going to do with the rest of your life? How are you going to make things better for you? Will you walk in the path that was chosen for you?

I want to be better than I was yesterday and every day I vow to learn something new. I vow to fight for my right to be happy and free. Today and this day forward I will honor who I am and whose I am. While continually giving thanks for not allowing myself to be bound by the lack of knowledge. Being devoid of over standing is not an option. We hold these truths once we obtain them to be self-evident that yes all men are created equal, but they are not and I mean not treated equal. Once you can grasp that concept, then you can move forward in a way that leaves you with a sense of purpose and freedom. A portion of these words come from the U.S. Constitution.

Here are the exact words from the second chapter of the U.S. Constitution; **"We hold these truths to be self-evident, that all men are created equal, that they are endowed by their Creator with certain unalienable Rights, that among these are Life, Liberty and the pursuit of Happiness. — That to secure these rights, Governments are instituted among Men, deriving their just powers from the consent of the governed, — That whenever any Form of Government becomes destructive of these ends, it is the Right of the People to alter or to abolish it, and to institute new Government, laying its foundation on such principles and organizing its powers in such form, as to them shall seem most likely to effect their Safety and Happiness."**

We as a people need to study even that because we live in a country that we really have no knowledge of what certain rights mean for us. We do not utilize these rights because we don't know them. We must study to show ourselves approved in every area of our lives.

Kuumba (Creativity): To do always as much as we can, in the way we can, in order to leave our community more beautiful and beneficial than we inherited it.

I know that some would say that it is meaningless to work to clean up something that is just going to get messed up again, but I disagree. We can make a difference and we must. If you live in an area that needs some repairs or cleaning, please do your part. I know that some, well a vast majority don't care, but then there are people like us that do. It is the small things that really do make a difference, like not littering. Use the trash cans, they are there for a reason.

I know that this seems like common sense but trust me, it is not for some. Let's just face it that some people are just nasty and lazy. That is why it is imperative that we as a people teach our children that it is not okay to be nasty. I don't care if you own the house that you live in or renting it, you must take care of it. Keep it clean and make the necessary repairs. Take pride in your neighborhoods by doing your part to keep it clean and orderly.

This land is God's land that He has allowed us to inhabit. Therefore, it is our responsibility to do our part to ensure that it is safe and clean. Yes, I know that it is not an easy job when we have so much destruction around us, but I know that it all starts with one step at a time. I will not do a long drawn out piece about the benefits of cleanliness because common sense or not, filth is just that, filth.

Imani (Faith): To trust with all our hearts in God, our people, our parents, our teachers, our leaders, and the righteousness and victory of our struggle.

The word faith means many things to many people because we are all vastly different. It is the faith that is within us that compels us to move forward when everything in our lives seem to be standing still. It is faith that makes the impossible possible. To trust in that which we can't see is a mighty powerful thing. Everything starts in the mind first. If you can think it, then it is so. That's why it is important to meditate and ponder on the things that you dream of. It is not a good thing to be thoughtless. It literally scares me when a person asks another individual what are you thinking, and that person replies "nothing." I can't even fathom in my mind not having a thought because I am always thinking, even in my sleep. My brain never takes a break. I am always thinking and study. Reasoning and relating. I have faith that this too shall pass. That I will complete the task that God has so graciously set before me. It is through my thoughts that I am able to get up with hope. I have faith. Yes, I do, regardless of the amount. Everyday whether in the face of adversity or calmness, I am exercising my faith. "**Hebrews 11**" says it all.

It is written in the word that we are His and created in His image and likeness. So we must begin to operate in that fact. There is no longer a need for excuses nor the blame game. We are who we are, and we must do what is required to get to where we as a people need to be. My prayer is that whoever is reading this is learning from all that the Almighty has allowed me to write and that these words become an eye opener for those who aren't aware of what has been written.

The incorporation of biblical scripture is important to me because I am a child of God, and I am operating in the will of the Most High. What I write must line up with the word of God. Scripture is a present help for me in my time of need, and I pray that it is for you as well. However, if for whatever reason you are not aware of the Holy Bible I pray that through this you become aware and seek it in its entirety.

Find someone who can be of service to you in your quest to gain a better overstanding of whom you are through the eyes of God. Someone who can teach you how to study the word and apply it to your life, and therefore, make things better for you.

There is comfort in the arms of the Lord if you allow Him into you circumstances. He will be everything that you need Him to be for you, but you have to make the first steps toward your relationship with him. God loves you and yes I know that I have told you this before, and I will also tell you this again and again until you absorb it. God is bigger than your circumstances and better than any man-made fix. Just lean on Him and not your own overstanding of who and what you are and going through.

« 25 » MOVING FORWARD WITH GOD'S COVERING

STARTING EACH DAY WITH a prayer is a great way to give balance to the day. Taking a few moments to fellowship and talk with God is a must when you are working towards bettering any relationship whether it is with self, others, and most importantly God. There are going to be moments when everything that you do will appear to be a failure and during those moments, you are going to have to dig in deep to that holy place where you can find rest in order to make it through those moments.

The closer you get to God the hard things are going to appear to be for you because that is the way that Satan what's it to appear but I say to you to hold on to God's unchanging hands and know that He will never leave you nor forsake you. I am not here to discourage only to encourage and make you aware that by taking up the cross you will have the enemy coming after you with everything that they have. Just know that God also has assigned to you a fleet of warring angels to fight on your behalf.

You are not alone no matter what it may seem like. The spirit of the Lord is always there. Keep in mind that no matter what happens that the truth shall make you free. There is freedom in knowing what God told you and holding on to that truth at all costs. There will be those who will come along and try to deceive you. Yes, even those who have been in your midst all along. Those that are closest to you will be the ones that will be used against you.

They will be the ones that will have a greater distaste for the change that they see in you. It is sad, but oh so true. There are people who have been in your midst all of your life who will now speak against that which God is doing for you and through you, but I say to you that you must not now, nor ever, allow what others say sway you from the will of God over your life. This walk nor this battle will be an easy one, but it has already been done and won by El Shaddai.

There is nothing that God can't do for you if you open your heart to Him. I feel sad when I look back over my life at the people who are no longer with me but then I cry and look at what God has done for me and where I am now in my relationship with him.

I had to give up some things in order to gain a greater perspective on who God is and who I am in Him. Am I flawed? Yes. Have I arrived at that pivotal moment where I know everything, and I do not need assistance from anyone? No. The point that I am trying to make is that I will always be in need of improvement as long as I am in this fleshly body. I have made many mistakes, and I am still making them but the difference between then and now is that I am learning from those mistakes far quicker than I use too.

We must still remember as women of Christ that we are the glory of God and nothing and no one can take that away from us. We must at all times keep in mind that God sees us for who we are no matter what we are doing or have done because He knows our heart. There is nothing that we have done that God doesn't know about, and there is nothing that He can't deliver us from. You must trust in the Lord and know that without a shadow of a doubt that He has us covered on all sides and at all times.

Choosing your battle is key when dealing with your enemies. There is nothing more important than your wellbeing whether that be physical, spiritual, or mental. You have a right to be happy, free, and safe. Don't allow anyone to tell you otherwise. No one on this earth deserves to be mistreated, and you have a right to feel good about yourself. Positive self - imagine is imperative to your daily survival because how you view yourself is vital to you coming out of whatever trial you are in at this moment.

You must get in the mirror every day and tell yourself that you are loved, beautiful, anointed, and treasured because you are. Yes, you are because God sees you in this way because you are His. A wise man told me on more than one occasion that I must learn to forgive myself, and I share this same advice with you. When you have been abused and mistreated, you tend to blame yourself. You tend to take responsibility for the actions of those who have misused you.

In your mind, you somehow think that if you would have done something different that this tragic event would never have happened but that can't be further from the truth because most things that are tragic are beyond our control. The old adage that sometimes bad things happen to good people is so very true. However, don't fall into that statistical trap and allow others to dictate how you are going to turn out just because you came from a certain place or because you have had to endure some horrific events. When you are a child of God, no one can truly place you anywhere that God doesn't want you to be. You must at all times think positive thoughts and stop giving other people power over your emotions.

Every time someone knows that they can make you go against what God has placed over your life they will. You are going to continue to come against resistance because of whose you are. No matter where you go or what you do God has and always will be the author and the finisher of all things. There is nothing that God can't handle on your behalf but you must allow Him in to do so. He is just waiting on you to make the next move so that He can come in and repair all that is damaged and please allow Him the allotted amount of time to heal you because all of this damage didn't just happen overnight.

Healing is a process. Oh yes, I know what you are

thinking and yes God can do it at a blink of an eye, but sometimes He just wants you to go through the process. Yes, some healings are miraculous while others are done in intervals and only God can decide how it's going to be done. We would like to think that we are the ones in control but truthfully only God has the power to control everything on earth and in the heavens. We do get to make choices and sometimes those choices are lead to be made by what we see, hear, and do. There are times when the words and actions of others move us to make choices that we otherwise would not have made.

You must be careful about doing things and making decisions when you are angry and influenced by outside forces. No choices should be made when you are in the heat of anger, frustration, nor pressure. If you have a decision to make and the circumstances aren't right for the proper decision to be made, then take a step back from it and reflect upon whatever it is and be realistic about that decision and proceed with caution.

When making choices in the heat of the moment do to emotions we tend to mess things up worse and on the flip side of that over analyzing can cause just as much damage because you can over-think a situation and miss an opportunity for reconciliation. It is all about balance in every area of our lives and knowing when to let go verses when to hold on, because some things just aren't meant to be fixed. The Bible even speaks about there is a time for everything, and there are times when you have to just walk away, but then there are times when we must fight.

"To whom much is given much is required." The more knowing that you have, the more responsibility it carries. You can't keep learning key information and not think that it is not going to be used at some point in your lives. The studying and the praying and the fasting and the sacrifices are all for a reason, nothing just happens, whether you know it or not. There's a reason behind and in front of everything.

God doesn't do anything just because and for every problem He has already created a solution. We must learn that in all things there is a purpose and that there is always hope. You must know yourself because God knows you. Yes, it is hard and yes, there is still a lot to do and no, it is not fair. However, with all that you have done and have been done to you, God is still and will forever be able to do, **"exceedingly and abundantly above all that you can think and hope for."**

One day, we will be able to look past all that has happened and see the greater good in all of this. One day, those tears of sadness will be replaced with tears of joy. One day, the madness will be transformed into gladness. I know because I know the God that I serve. The God that has me clothed in my right mind and able to still move with all that I have gone through.

« 26 » BACKWARDS

THERE COMES A MOMENT in this life when one must look back at all that has been, so that one must know where one is going. Study who you are and what you have gone through, as to not repeat the cycle of destruction that you have been traveling in. We have discussed this before, and now I will go into greater detail about why this is imperative and who you should be looking back to. We must know his-story and why it is the reason we are where we are today as a whole. We must look at those who have sacrificed and fought for the cause. We must then know our place in this war against our spirits.

Yes, I said spirits because this here is a spiritual war waged against us by demonic forces. We do not wrestle against flesh and blood. **"We wrestle against principalities and the rulers of darkness."** This is a Holy war, and we must be better prepared for our role in this. Yes, the battle is the Lords for those of you who know your word. However, we are not to lay dormant while the Angels in the heavenlies are fighting on our behalf. There are steps that we must take in order to ensure that our roles are being fully covered.

The word says to, **"study to show thyself approved."** Yes, you must study your enemies as well as yourself. You must study the reasons why these things have been allowed to happen. You must have a clear overstanding as to the weapons and tools needed and used in this war. We must as a people, learn ways to effectively organize our time and stop making excuses as to why we can't do something and start figuring out ways in which we can. We must become better equipped in this thing called life and realize just how precious, it really is. **"For life is but a vapor that soon passes away."**

Time is the most valuable resource that we as human beings have on this earth. So, therefore, we must use it wisely because we all get the same amount to work with on a daily bases, and that's 24 hours. Yes, 24 hours! What are you doing with the 24 hours that you were given today? Are you bored? If the answer to this is a yes, then you are not effectively utilizing the time in which God has so graciously given you because if you were you wouldn't use such a foolish sentence because there is too much to learn to be bored as a human being.

Read a book, help the elderly, clean up your neighborhood, watch a documentary, volunteer, etc. See, there is plenty to do. Using your brain is one of the most important things in the world to do. Exercise that muscle. It really needs it. Analyze and study those things and people that are around you. Don't be fooled or mocked by those who get angry because you want to know things about them. See, their defensive because they have something to hide. When someone gets an attitude about you wanting to know more about them, then you need to look even deeper.

Think about this, you have a right to know who is in your life. You have a right to investigate any potential friend, lover, spouse, employee, etc. because we live in an age where deception runs rampant. However, we also live in an age where it is easier to find out certain things about people as well. There is nothing wrong with taking precautions.

By the time you get through studying all these aspects of your life, you won't have time for foolishness nor boredom. There is still plenty to do when you are a servant of the Most High God. It is always best to know what and who you are dealing with in every area of your life. Yes, I know that you will never know everything about a person or even a situation but not even trying to learn is total foolishness. Even the word says seek, and ye shall find. If you look hard enough, whatever information you need will be revealed.

I know that first hand, just as well as whatever you are searching for ask God to reveal it and to be your strength to deal with whatever it is that will be revealed. The word says that, **"the truth shall make you free,"** and that's exactly what it will do, so you had better be prepared for all that the truth, that you are seeking will bring. I know all too well what truth will do because when something is hidden the subconscience will always let you know that something is not right.

The mind and spirit are very powerful, and they are two totally different areas of our life that are supposed to work in conjunction to one another, but we know wholeheartedly that sometimes this is not the case. The mind often than not wants what the Spirit fights against. Our spirits are our direct link to the Most High God and our spirits work continuously to keep us in alignment with whose we are but because of the flesh that we are so beautifully wrapped in, we tend to end up fighting that which is best for us.

This flesh can literally keep us from achieving what God has set in place for us if we do not learn to deny ourselves in certain areas. This walk with God is full of sacrifices, and if you don't take that into account, you have failed before you have begun. No one that takes up the cross and follows the path that God has set before them will come out of this unchanged.

Change is inevitable when you walk with God, and you shouldn't expect to remain the same when you are in the presence of the Almighty. The seconds change into minutes, the minutes change into hours, the hours change into days, the days, change into weeks, the weeks change into months, and the months change into years. I say all of that to say this, then what makes you think that you will not change?

People who sit up and complain about people who have changed are sad because nothing in this lifetime stays the same. Life is about growth and evolution. If you are not evolving, then that means that you are stagnant and being stagnant is never a good thing. If you are one of those people who have a problem with change, then you must learn that growth is a must and to embrace that which you have a problem with. Don't misunderstand me now because the change that I am speaking of is the positive kind.

I will never condone anyone changing for the negative because positive change is the only change that is to be fought to achieve. Growth is positive. So, therefore, please strive for that which is positive. Excel in all areas. Always keep in mind that growth is a process and that it takes time. No, I don't know how much time it will take you to heal from all that has happened to you, but I do know that if you keep moving in a positive direction that change will come.

Yes, you will still have moments when you feel as if you can't go on. Yes, you will question everything that you are doing and have done. Yes, you will feel like it's not worth the effort. Yes, everything that you are feeling is a natural part of the healing process. Everything that you are feeling is okay, and you have a right to feel whatever it is that you are feeling at any moment that you are feeling it. You must always give birth to your feelings because it is a part of your healing process. If you feel like screaming, then do it because that is a release. Allow yourself that freedom to expel everything that needs to come out of you. Keep in mind that this is for your betterment and no one has the right to tell you that your feelings aren't valid. I know all too well what it is like to walk around pretending that everything is okay when it is not. I even named myself the great pretender. I would hold my head up high and act as if I didn't have a problem in this world nor any pain to go along with it.

I never asked anyone for anything, not even prayer. I relied solely on me at one point because I wasn't even giving over anything to God because I felt unworthy. Yes, I felt unworthy of anything that God had to offer me so I would not ask, not even for forgiveness. At one point in my life, I felt empty and defeated as if nothing that I did or was doing would matter to anyone. That my effort was in vain and fruitless. Even as my anointing grew, I still felt this way, and there was nothing that I could do to stop it.

I would pray and study and worship, then right afterwards I would cry and condemn myself. I would look back over my life and all the mistakes that I had made and scream out to God, why? Why had I, this anointed, intelligent, appointed woman of God been so misguided, misled, and mishandled? I had allowed myself to be betrayed and hurt. I took and still do take full ownership of what I have allowed to happen to me because of my disobedience to God.

I have not just started my journey in the kingdom of the Most High. So, therefore, I know that there are things that I brought upon myself because I wasn't living according to the will of God. That in itself is a very painful revelation. I, even now, in my moments of reflection, cringe at all that I have gone through in the name of love, only to realize that it was not love after all because contrary to popular beliefs love is not painful. Love is life, freedom, joy, building, and sacrificial.

Love is not just a word or a verb as some would say. Love is about looking deep within a person's soul and pouring the greatest part of yourself into them. Love is not used in conjunction with but, love just is.

You do not take away from love by demeaning, belittling, abusing, and killing off the very one that you claim to love. On this quest to find my one true love I have found that most people who walk the face of the earth do not know what true love is and that most have not even received love, therefore, most do not know how to give love. Love is like a magnet. It gravitates to that which is like itself.

Love is often confused with lust or limerence. It is imperative that we learn what love is, in order to identify or recognize what love truly is. Everyone on this earth needs love to function in the manner in which God designed us to function. Love has everything to do with everything. It is a proven fact that those that are loved are healthier and more vibrant than those that are not. It is also a fact that love and I mean true love, heals and nurtures.

Love in itself is a medicine. Love makes you feel alive and able to conquer that which has bound you. Love gives hope to the otherwise hopeless. Love transcends boundaries that would otherwise seem impossible to achieve. Love is everything to me because my one true love is God. He is and has always been the one that I have been seeking, even when I was not aware, that's what I was doing. I did not even overstand what I was doing or even why I was so unhappy in areas of my life where I knew that I should have been joyful. It was because I was missing that which was going to complete me. I have even in my quest to prepare for my Divine Partner put a standard on even him. That some would say is unattainable, but I beg to differ. God knows that I need a Divine Partner that has God seeping out of his pores.

When you have been touched by the Most High God your standards for human's change, you began to look for the Holy Spirit in everyone that you come in contact with, and when you don't see it then you feel a sense of disappointment. You began to crave the touch that only the spirit can give and when you don't get that you become again disappointed. The touch of the spirit is like no other and when you do come into the knowing of who you are and whose you are, you can't help but to see things and people differently. You can't help but seek those who are like the spirit that dwells from the Most High.

People tend to downplay the Holy Spirit, that's if they even have knowledge of the power of the Holy Spirit. When you are a child of God's, you have certain expectations that you yourself work towards obtaining and those expectations you also have for others. I personally came into this revelation when I started to study who I am and when I did so, I began to realize that I had been cheating myself out of so much. There is no greater disappointment than that of disappointing yourself. When you know that without a shadow of a doubt that you have done this to yourself, you feel a sense of longing.

You can't help but to search, seek, and find that which has led you to your greater truth. Your greater you. There is something to be said about a person who chooses to see who they really are, versus a person who totally refuses to come face to face with the real them. It is the pretense in this world that keeps us bond because the average person wants to be someone that they are not. The average person has a warped imaged of themselves, so it is easier for them to pretend than to be real. Realism is something that the average human being can't cope with.

Webster defines realism as such:
1.concern for fact or reality and rejection of the impractical and visionary.
2. a: a doctrine that universals exist outside the mind; specifically: the conception that an abstract term names an independent and unitary reality.
B: a theory that objects of sense perception or cognition exist independently of the mind — compare nominalism.
3. the theory or practice of fidelity in art and literature to nature or to real life and to accurate representation without idealization.

Yes, you would think that being real is automatic. However, it is not, in this day and age that we now live in where it is easier to fake, pretend, and portray to be something and someone else. Society as a whole encourages pretense and most in society fall into that status quo. I have learned the very painful lesson of why it is done. When you are faced with the truth, that you, in fact, are doing this, you have to then make the painful choice to change this behavior which opens you up for another painful reality, and that is that you do not know how to be you. You don't even know who you are. You have walked around so long pretending to be someone or something else, so much so that when truth time comes you can't even differentiate between the two.

Oh, don't misunderstand me because we all at some point in our lives have pretended. Especially when we were children but the reality is that we are no longer children and some of us adults still are stuck in the state of pretense. The fact of the matter is, is that if you don't look at your reality, you won't even truly come into who God wants and needs you to be for the Kingdom. It is not about allowing your reality to bind you, it is about knowing the truth and taking that truth and allowing that truth to work for you.

The truth brings about a sense of freedom and the freedom to fix that which is broken is key in deliverance. Most don't want the responsibility of truth because truth forces change. Truth chokes the life out of lies, and most would rather live a lie than operate in the truth. It is a sad thing when you have a body of people who refuse to see who they are and whose they are and would rather walk around operating in a false sense of living. The false sense of knowing will bring about the greatest deception every done to ones-self, is to ones-self. Just because you refuse to see that which is true does not take away from the fact that truth is still out there. It just means that you refuse to acknowledge it. The truth is the truth whether you know it or not.

Just as pretending is still pretending. The difference with that is that deception is only realized once the truth is revealed. The truth, on the other hand, is still the truth whether you know it or not. You can be the greatest pretender and only you know the lies that you operate in but there is a God that knows all things, and He will make sure that His truth is revealed no matter how many lies have been told. No matter how deep the deception is or how long you have been pretending.

God is an awesome God, and He reigns from heaven to earth. There is no other like Him even if you decide to pretend that He doesn't exist still doesn't take away from the fact that He still does. God will not be mocked nor will He allow anyone or anything to take away from that which He is. He is and has always been present, Omni-present. I trust in Him, and I know that which dwells within me. I know that I am not here on this earth operating on my own accord.

I do not need anyone to tell me that He is real because I know that He is, especially every time my heart beats, I know that it is not due to anything that I have done. I know that when I have a thought, and my body moves, I know it is not due to anything that I have done. I know when the sun rises, and the sun sets it is not due to anything that anyone on this earth has done or is doing. It doesn't matter who you are or what degree you may hold, there are certain things that you will not be able to logically explain. God is not one that you can contain Him, and He does not think nor operate on a level that your small mind can even fathom. I love God, and I know that He loves me. I am thankful for all that He has done and is doing in my life. I have not arrived as I stated before and I am fine with that knowing. I know that as long as I am on this earth that I am in a transitional phase that will never end. It is for me about evolution for the betterment of the Kingdom of The Most High God, and I will not stop learning nor teaching for those who want that truth, and I will not stop pressing toward God's truth. I know that challenges will still come, and I know that haters will too, but I rest in the fact that God is who I live for and when I die He is also who I die for.

I have learned in this life that no matter what I do I will never be able to please man and I am not going to try. I am seeking to please God, and I am doing that daily by remaining faithful and knowing that He will do what He says that He will do in my life. The Bible says that **"without faith it is impossible to please God."** I am not perfect, but I am definitely on my quest to please God. There is nothing pretentious about the God that I serve, and I love that, **"He will never leave me nor forsake me,"** even when I don't have a full overstanding of what is happening in my life.

There are times when I question that which is happening to me and wonder what is the purpose for all of this. No one will ever have all the answers, and there will be moments when you question your very existence because you are human, and God doesn't mind you asking Him questions that you legitimately don't have the answers to. He wants you to enquire about what you have no knowledge of. He wants you to seek the truth no matter what the reasons may be.

It is up to you to decide what is necessary in your life. What is it that you require for your health and well-being and then to seek that which you have discovered to be what is deem important to you. We all have needs but just as different as our personalities, so are some of our needs. Yes, we all have some basic commonalities like; love, shelter, clothing, food, etc., but it is the differences in other areas, that make us unique. It is our uniqueness that we should always embrace because it is what is needed in this earth for diversity. It would be a rather mundane place if we all were exactly the same.

I love the fact that I am uniquely made and that there is not another human being on this earth that is exactly like me. Then on the flip side of that spectrum, I am thankful to God for similarities because knowing and interacting with others who have similar views and interests as I do is a good thing. These similarities are what makes some people get along and co-habitat with one another. It ensures that certain issues don't have to be a problem. Common interests and goals are a must when in a relationship because it allows the partners to spend more quality time together doing the things that they have in common.

There are a lot of things that we can do in intimate relationships that can keep down a lot of problems if we would make better choice when it comes to choosing a mate. Finding someone who has similar qualities, interest, goals, and dreams as yourself will make for a happier relationship. We cause ourselves undue stress by making the wrong choices in mates. We sometimes innocently think that these will grow on us or that we can somehow mold them into what we want in a mate, and that can't be further from the truth.

The fact of the matter is as I have stated before, you do not have the ability to change anyone because you are not God. What you can do is find someone who is close to what you want in a mate and accept them for who they are. Embrace your similarities and acknowledge your differences. Know that no two people will always agree or get along. Know that this is a normal part of life. Learn to be realistic with yourself and others because we are all flawed and accepting your flaws is called growth.

Once you have accepted your flaws, then you can start working on accepting others. It is okay to be different, and it is even better being you. You are uniquely built, and you shouldn't want to be like anyone else.

« 27 » KNOWING THE FEMALE BODY

IT AMAZES ME WHEN I talk with other women and find out that they do not know what they should about their own bodies and it is even sad that they are even fearful about learning about their own bodies because they have been taught that it is wrong. Especially the older women. I write this chapter because as redundant as it may seem, it is truly needed.

We live in a time where you would think that this is common, but it is not. There are females walking this earth without even knowing that they menstruate and urinate from two different holes. Yeah, I know that this may be graphic for some, but it is needed by most.

We must learn about our bodies so that we can teach our daughters about their bodies. Knowledge again is power. In knowing about who you are and whose you are, you will gain a better perspective as to how you need to be treated by yourself, and therefore, by others.

It is imperative that we as a whole find a way to come together and share what we have learned with the unlearned. No two females are exactly alike, but we are similar individuals who share the basic parts of anatomy with one another. Learning what's considered to be normal versus what's considered to be abnormal is what will empower us with the tools needed to became more effective women. Whether it is discussing our genitalia or our emotions, it is what is needed for a better overstanding of what is to come in reference to our bodies.

In order to teach someone else what is pleasurable to you, you must know what is pleasurable to you. You learn this by exploring. Know that it is okay to touch your own body. No, I am not talking about masturbation. I am speaking of the human touch. Whether it is rubbing lotion on your skin, lathering soap on your body, or just simply massaging your own feet. Please know that is okay to take the time to feel your own touch and accept that it feels good too.

There is nothing perverse or wrong in doing so, even if some of you have been taught that it is wrong. We as women give our partners more control over our own bodies than we have. It is not them who should tell us what is pleasurable to us. On the contrary, it is us who should tell them what we like. However, that is an impossible task for any partner when you don't know yourself.

We are human beings require the human touch and

to know this information alone is powerful. Do you know that there is healing in the human touch? We are built to be entered and there is nothing wrong with that but there is a right way and a wrong way to do everything. So ladies, be careful about how you allow your partners to enter your bodies and be mindful of how they behave once they are inside.

Be protective of your reproductive system and your vagina because rough intercourse does more damage than you realize. It can cause major medical problems for you, now and even later. Our bodies are our temple, and we should treat them accordingly. Yes, I know to each its own and that every woman has a right to her own. All I am saying is that more than often when pain is involved in an area that is supposed to be pleasurable and the only way you can get off is through extreme pain and torture, then there is something seriously wrong.

Most women who have been abused use pain as a catalyst to get off. They somehow feel empowered when the pain is inflicted upon them, and some feel as if they need the pain because it is the only feeling that they feel that they deserve because of the past abuse.

If pain has become your pleasure, then you need to take a moment and examine why? Ask yourself and be prepared for the answer that your subconscious is going to give you. The mind is a wonderful tool, and this wonderful tool can sometimes malfunction especially when trauma has happened to an individual. The human body is amazing, and it will do some extraordinary things in order to protect itself and to survive.

The key here is to become aware of why we do what we do and to ensure that what we are doing is for the benefit of our health, well-being, and happiness. As women, we hold so much power, that if we aren't mindful and walking in the knowing of whom we are, that power can become useless. You must first know who you are in order to use the gifts that God has so graciously given to you.

Our bodies are magnificent, and no one on this earth should be allowed to mistreat it and we as women do a great disservice to ourselves when we do not stand firm on what we know to be right for us, whether that be collectively as a whole or individually. God created us to operate in the knowing of whose we are, and that is His. We are Empress's, Queen's, Princess's, Mother's, Daughter's, Wives, Goddess's. We are God's children, heirs to the throne of the Most High and we will no longer accept mistreatment from anyone especially, not ourselves.

For it is through the mistreatment of ourselves that we allow other's, to do so. We must stop this vicious cycle of abuse because it is not acceptable. El Shaddai has allowed us to be the carriers of His most precious gift. He allowed us to bring forth life. He created us last for a reason as it's because we are the best. He saved the best for last.

So stop allowing others to tell you that you are worthless because you aren't. You are priceless, and you are God's favor and whenever you marry, that favor is what that man obtains from the Most High because of you. Therefore, without you, there are certain things that God will not allow him to have, or do, or be. Oh darling, favor from God is an awesome thing, and not everyone obtains it. We have for so long been led astray by insecure little boys walking around in men's bodies.

When you do not know your worth, then you allow someone else to put a price on you, and they will always mark your value lower than what you are actually worth. Getting into the Word and allowing God to set the standard is the first step in correcting the errors from our past. Whether that past be 5 seconds ago or 5 years ago, there is still hope that things will change for the better, and that change starts with knowing your body.

Being a woman can sometimes be very complex especially when the key components that we require aren't set in place for us. Our bodies can so easily become unbalanced due to stress from our homes, jobs, and relationships with friends and family. That is why we must stop and take the necessary time to relax, rest, and rejuvenate ourselves. You would be amazed at how much better you will feel when you allow yourself some down time.

In your down time make sure that you are receiving the human touch. Allow your Divine Partner (if you have one) to make love to you because this is a part of your relaxation. Yes, it is. You must learn to allow him the chance to pamper you. If he doesn't know how, then teach him. A nice warm bath by candlelight followed by a full body massage with an elegant aromatic bottle of self-heating oil is just what's needed to get you back in balance with self.

Oh, ladies don't downplay the power of the human touch, especially when being made love to. See, when your Divine Partner is making love to you there is no room for selfishness on his part because he knows that that moment is all about you and your needs. It is his duty to cater to you. You are to allow room for pampering and release. We as women sometimes don't allow other's to take care of us because we are so use to doing for everyone else and forget that we too need to be nurtured.

Your Divine Partner is in your life to take the load off and to relieve some of the pressures of the day. He is to be your comfort zone. It is okay to let your guard down around him because his duty is to provide you with a way of escape from the discomforts of the world. We as women, especially those of us who have been abused, do not know how to let our guard down because it means that we would have to be vulnerable and with that comes fear. The fear of letting go and allowing another individual to see you without the barriers that you have so carefully placed around you in order to protect you from any further hurt and pain.

We as the nurturers of the world must learn to allow ourselves to be nurtured also. Pampered from our head to our toes, from the heart to the soul. We must learn that it is okay to let go. Letting go gives us a means of rejuvenation. It revitalizes us. It cleans the slate so to speak for a new start, the dawning of the coming anew is important in this walk with the Most High God because there are always things that will come along to throw you off balance, to deter us from the purpose.

Learning to take proper care of yourself is the key to living a healthier life. It starts with priorities, and you are your first priority because if you do not put yourself first, then you aren't going to be able to take care of anyone else. You must start this process from the inside out and make you rway from head to toe. For instance, are you in tune with your emotions? What does your inner being need and desire? Listen carefully for what your spirit is telling you because our spirit does communicate with us, we just tend to be so busy doing other things that we aren't listening until it's too late. Meditation is the key to becoming one with your spirit, being alone while praying and studying the word of God.

Once you are in tune with your spirit, then you can start working on your body and the first thing should be the head. What is going on in your head that needs to be handled? Are you having headaches, vision problems, ringing in the ears, mouth pain, depression, hearing voices, having flashbacks, etc.? You must examine yourself thoroughly and be honest with yourself about what you find and then take the necessary steps to fix it.

It is a sad reality that the average woman will not go to the dentist but will buy a designer purse or a pair of $100.00 gym shoes. I say this because it needs to be said. Your dental health is more important than rocking the latest purse or shoes. Do you know that an infection in your mouth can spread to other parts of your body if not treated? There are many things that can be going on in the body that will show up in the mouth. That's why it is important to pay attention to every aspect of your body, beginning with the top and working your way to the rest of your body, remember head to toes.

Okay, now that you get the picture about the head, now let's work our way a little further down. Your throat, yes, we tend to forget about the throat both inside and outside. Pay careful attention to the outside of the throat. Do you see any swelling? Feel your throat and do you feel any lumps, knots, soreness when touched. If so, you needed to quickly make an appointment with your primary care doctor. Ask to have your throat checked along with a thyroid panel because the thyroid (although a small gland in the neck) can cause your entire body to be thrown off balance and can cause other major organs to stop function properly. Thyroid problems, if gone untreated can cause reproductive problems, among other problems.

Stressed out, run down, exhausted? Weight issues? Feeling blue? Losing hair? These could be signs that your thyroid is out of whack. The two most common causes of thyroid disease in the U.S. - Hashimoto's disease and Graves' disease – these are also both autoimmune diseases. Many women do not realize how important the thyroid function is until it stops functioning properly. Even your iodine intake is more important than you realize because that too can cause the thyroid to malfunction. Iodine -- which is ingested from food and supplements -- is a building block for the production of thyroid hormones. Sufficient iodine is particularly important during early pregnancy when the brain development of the fetus relies on the mother's intake of iodine and thyroid status.

Now that we have discussed the neck let's get started on the chest. From the bones right below your neck to the breast, you must touch and examine because it is important to check for lumps, swelling, tenderness, and pain. Do you have chest pains when breathing, running, exercising? If so, you need to make an appointment with your primary care doctor so that he can help you figure out what is going on with your body.

Now the all to unspoken breast examine that most women do not feel the need to do because for whatever reason they think that it is not neccessary, or they aren't comfortable touching their own breast. Well, you had better get over yourself and do those self-breast examines to make sure that you do not have any discharge from the nipples or abnormal lumps or growths there and if you do get your butt to the doctor and schedule a mammogram.

A mammogram is an x-ray of the breast. A diagnostic mammogram is used to diagnose breast disease in women who have breast symptoms or an abnormal result on a screening mammogram. Screening mammograms are used to look for breast disease in women who are asymptomatic; that is, those who appear to have no breast problems. Screening mammograms will usually take two views (x-ray pictures taken from different angles) of each breast while diagnostic mammograms may take more views of the breast.

Once you have made sure you breast are okay you can now move on to the heart. Does your heart beat properly because if it doesn't trust me when I say that you will know? Whether it is heart palpitations (racing or pounding of the heart), arrhythmia (irregular heart beat or skipping), bradycardia (your heart beats very slowly), or some other form of heart disease it is serious and needs to be checked out. Do not dismiss signs and symptoms as nothing because it may be something life threatening.

The most common heart attack symptoms in women is some type of pain, pressure or discomfort in the chest. But it's not always severe or even the most prominent symptom, particularly in women. Women are more likely than men to have heart attack symptoms unrelated to chest pain, such as Neck, shoulder, upper back or abdominal discomfort, shortness of breath, nausea or vomiting, sweating, lightheadedness or dizziness, unusual fatigue.

Although these aren't all of the symptoms as some do vary from person to person but these are the most common. Also, do note that if you are having crushing pain in your chest and problems breathing do not hesitate to call 911. Remember that a healthy heart is a happy heart.

We have now made it to the stomach. Is your stomach bloated, upset, gassy, cramping, or hurting? Well if the answer to any of these is yes, then you need to figure out what the cause is and in doing so, you will find that even the simplest of things can throw the stomach off balance. How we handle stress is a very important part of our daily lives because if not handled properly, stress can cause major health problems and even death. We must be mindful of peptic ulcers, gallstones, acid reflux, irritable bowel syndrome, Crohn's disease, and more stomach disorders. Pay close attention to that upset stomach and that burning sensation.

Now that we have had a briefing on the stomach let's go a little bit lower to the reproductive system. Again stress, heavy lifting, and excessive exercising can cause a malfunction of the female reproductive system. Everything that we do or don't do can cause a reaction in our bodies. The vagina itself undergoes many changes during the month. First of all, the vagina is supposed to be a place of moisture, therefore, it does secrete. A vaginal discharge is actually normal, and it does change throughout the month going from light clear mucus too thick milky white.

Each discharge is meant to be and for a reason, for instance, the clear mucus can be a sign of pending ovulation and the milky white can be a sign that you have a healthy vagina and is in a certain time during the cycle process. As long as your discharge is not green, gray, yellow and foul smelling, itching, or burning you are good. Also, during your menstruation write down your flow and start and stop time every month because this is important information that is always needed during doctor visits.

Also, be mindful of excessive bleeding during your menstruation because it may be a sign of hormonal problems or other medical problems. Excessive bleeding can lead to anemia. Never dismiss excessive bleeding as nothing, you could be hemorrhaging, and that can be deadly. No two females are exactly alike so what is a normal flow for you, may not be for the next woman, however if you are soaking a pad or tampon every hour then that is a need for concern and if so, you should get to your nearest emergency room.

There is also the need to clean properly, and I know that you are thinking "who is she to tell me to clean my vagina?" Well, ladies, it is a fact that most women only wash the outer lips of the vagina and never open up the lips and cleanse the inner portion. It is normal for the vagina to cleanse itself. There are some women who require a little extra help when normal washing and the natural cleansing process isn't enough or shall I say not effective. Then douching is required and if that doesn't get rid of the offensive odor, then you should quickly schedule an appointment with your gynecologist because the vagina is not supposed to have an offensive odor.

Being gentle is important when cleaning your vaginal area because excessive scrubbing is not necessary and can lead to infection, just as wiping from back to front after defecating. The rule is to wipe from front to back in order to prevent fecal matter from coming in contact with the vaginal area to ensure that there is no contamination that can again lead to infection.

Alright, let's continue on our journey to the least likely to discuss topic, that is the rectum. Yes, ladies we do sometimes encounter problems in this area, whether it is hemorrhoids, constipation, diarrhea, or gas, it needs to be addressed. Having regular bowel moments is important because an improper functioning colon is not a good thing. No two people again are alike, but you should be having a bowel moment every day if you are a meat eater and vegetarians, for us vegans at least twice daily. The body must rid itself of waste in order to keep us healthy. It's really a must to dispose of what the body no longer needs. Without this daily extraction, our bodies began to set up toxicity, and this leads to health issues and illness.

A lot of women take it lightly when they are constipated, simply dismissing it as nothing when in all actuality, it is a major deal. Just as on the flip side of that, having too many bowel movements can be just as dangerous because diarrhea can lead to dehydration. The body needs fluids to function properly and when you are losing more fluids than you intake, then that becomes a problem. Not only do you need to keep the body hydrated but make sure you are hydrating with mostly water and not overloading on sugary and caffeinated drinks.

Clean water is vital to the overall health of the body as we are about 60 percent water. Our bodies lose a lot of water during the day, especially when we are very active. Water is lost when you sweat, urinate, defecate, and cry. Therefore, it is imperative to constantly replace that which is lost. Hydration and fiber are the keys to a healthy colon. Remember illuminating waste is just as important as nourishing the body. Everything and I mean everything is about balance, and you must learn what your balance is because again no two human beings are exactly alike. Yes, we all have similarities, but it is up to each individual person to find out what is best for them in every area of their lives.

Our bodies are finely tuned instruments created by God, and we are supposed to take especially good care of them. However, there are times when we do damage this beautiful gifts from God. Our bodies are amazing, and they function so beautifully when they are in tune the way they were created to be. It amazes me when I think about how the veins run throughout our bodies and allows blood to flow through as our hearts pump this blood to and fro. Wow, God is awesome. We are the ultimate machine, and nothing can compare to it.

Whether it is the knowing that our skin is an organ or that our teeth aren't solid. Knowing is half the battle. For using what you have learned is just as important as learning. What you do with the information that you obtain is completely up to you and vital to your very existence. Not knowing something can be just as bad as knowing and not using it. So don't fall prey to the trap that you aren't held accountable for what you don't know because what you don't know can actually kill you.

I have learned that everything is a learning experience and that most learning experiences can be very painful. With all that we have encountered, whether willingly or unwillingly can be beneficial to us if we allow it to be. Lessons are all around us, and we can make the choice to stay stuck or press forward. Take care of yourselves and put yourself first when it comes to caring because if you don't care for you first, no one else will.

Nothing in this lifetime is more important than you and as soon as you realize that, then everything else is going to fall in place. Leaders must learn how to lead by example. So with that being said be mindful of your health.

« 28 » AFRICA THE MOTHERLAND

THERE ARE TIMES WHEN we think we know a fact, when that knowing is actually, a not knowing. Africa first off is a CONTINENT, not a country. I know that you may be saying, I know that and so does everyone else on this planet. Well, you are wrong because everyone on this planet doesn't know that Africa is a continent, let alone is also considered to be The Mother Land. Africa the continent has roughly 54 countries with in it.

I have decided to take a moment to take a closer look at Africa, and its biblically significant role to the World. As well as its economic role to the World in these modern or shall I say current times. Africa has a very rich history that extends to the beginning of time. From its rich land to its Royal Legacy. Africa has given birth to legendary leaders, Kings, Queens, Holy Warriors that has since passed on but whose contribution to this world still lives on. It however still holds some of the most Spiritually gifted people on this planet, who worship The Most High God and fight the spiritual battles in a way that surpasses what modern societies deem Holy.

There is a big misconception about African and her people. I first read about Africa when I was a child growing up in the South. Back when playing church included your best Sunday dress and a quarter for your offering. They had preachers that wheezed when they shouted out what they considered to be the word of God, trying to move the crowd in order to get a better offering. Many of them could not read, so they simply quoted what they often times heard the previous preacher say and somehow perfected the pretense.

They carried bibles and professed to be men of God sent on a mission to help those poor and needy come to the Kingdom of God. Well, it was during those times that I would pick up the bible and scroll through trying to make sense of it all. As I am still this day reading it and studying it and searching for the truth in the midst of all else. I have been through it in its entirety, and as I grow in my faith walk, I am given a fresh revelation about what I have previously read. Especially about the Garden of Eden and its location, which is for lack of a better word phenomenal.

This information has over the years taken me on a quest to find out as much as I could about The Garden of Eden and all that it represents to me. The mystery itself is amazing to say the least because as I would say the truth is right in front of your face, and it all starts from in the beginning. Yes, in the book of Genesis chapter 2, it gives a detailed description of where Yahweh walked. Whether debated or not, it is there for the knowing, for those of you who want the knowing.

It is absolutely astonishing to me that no matter what man tries to hide YHWH will still have the truth stand out. There is listed in the bible four rivers in the **"Garden of Eden; Pishon, Gihon, Tigris, and Euphrates."** Now as man would have it, they claimed that either the two rivers where metaphoric or that if they were real, they were destroyed in the Biblical flood. However, I find it rather interesting that only two of the four rivers that flowed from the Garden of Eden were quote on quote destroyed or existence were in question.

It is what I deem to be the two most important rivers that flowed from the garden that are mysteriously left out of the equation. The Scripture, however, gives great detail as to the locations of these first two rivers, although man says they are no longer there, if they were real. They have yet to explain why the latter two are still there and why YHWH didn't destroy those. If He, in fact, did eliminate the first two rivers.

My theory is that the first two rivers are still very much in existence and that the information is being purposely withheld from the mainstream for a reason. I find it very ironic that the wars of the world are always, and I mean always fought on what is deemed to be the Holy Land.

These wars have never been about money, oil, gold,

diamonds, nor people. It has and will always be about the Holy Land and who holds the key to that territory because of what it represents in the Spirit Realm and not in the natural, per say.

This is the Land where YWHW walked and interacted with man. This is the land of the true original man who **"YHWH breathe the breath of life in his nostrils after fashioning him from the dust of the ground."** It was only when YHWH breath in the nostrils of man that he became a living being. So, therefore, it is that very same breath that dwells within us right now in present day.

It is His Spirit that lives within us, His children. With this knowing, we must realize that He also left with us the power of discernment. You can feel within you when you are near the Holy truth and when you are in the company of a demonic lie.

The positive and the negative must exist in order for there to be balance in this realm. It should be expected, for good and evil will always exist because of the Father. Abba will not unequally yoke anything. Balance is a must, so you being deceived into thinking that only two of the Holy rivers exist in current times is for me expected. It is those half-truths that give life to the whole lies.

That is how the enemy can continue to deceive you by always placing some truth in with the lie because he knows that if you do search you will only scratch the surface. Once the average person scratches the surface and find that top layer to be the truth, they will automatically trust the rest of the information without checking any further.

Alright, now back to the rivers that flowed from the river in the Garden of Eden and formed four headwaters. The first river is the Pishon, which winds through Havilah. Which is located in East Africa.

There are always going to be the nay-sayings who will say that it is not so. They have their opinion about what did and didn't exist, and I am okay with that because everyone has a right to their own opinion.

According to the Holy Bible, The Most High walked the earth with the inhabitants. It also gives a detailed description of where He walked with them in Africa. Again this information in "**Genesis 2.**" Therefore, you can also deduce that The Garden of Eden is also in Africa as the description is the same as to where He walked. It is rather easy to see when you look at the location in the Holy Bible. Now as far as why these river heads are no longer on the current world maps and where the Garden of Eden is located in this current day. I say in the same place that it was then, in the biblical days.

Just because you can't see something doesn't mean that it is not there, nor does it mean that it doesn't exist. The Garden of Eden is still where it was then, and it is still protected as it was then. YHWH knows what type of people inhabit this earth, and He has made it plain to all who wants to see the Truth.

That garden contains all that is needed to heal the

people in this land, and as long as we remain a divided people, the multitude will forever fail to see the truths about why we are here and what our purpose for being here is. It is and has always been about the coming together of the people of YHWH.

Unity done in the operation of Love transforms all circumstances, and it even reveals the truth hidden amongst the lies. Man has been known to remove from the pages that which is known to be the truth as to further promote a lie. However, the truth still remains and can never be changed. **"Seek and ye shall find."**

« 29 » AT YOUR OWN PACE

ONE DAY WE ALL we get to a point where we are comfortable with who we are and whose we are and my prayer is that it happens at a time in our lives where we have plenty of time left to appreciate it. Nothing in this world can compare to that realization. We as a whole walk around this earth wondering who we are and for those of us that think that we know, are really lost. The vast majority are pretending that they know and placing judgment on those who admit that they are still working on figuring it out.

I know that this walk with God is a moment to moment walk for me. My walk is a constant journey towards betterment and growth in accordance to the spiritual me. The me that God says that I am without this fleshly body. I know that one day this life in this body will be over, and I am looking forward to being who God says that I am. I know that I am not perfect in this flesh, but I also know that I serve a God, who doesn't require that I be perfect. I know that there is a way out of whatever situation that I may have to face in this lifetime. I know that there is also hope that no matter what occurs God is and will always be on the throne.

One day I will be able to rest in the fact that all of my troubles will be over and until then I will keep praying, praising, and thanking God for His agape love towards me. I know that I can never do anything to earn His love and I know that He gives it to me freely. I trust in God wholeheartedly, and I do so not in spite of the things that have happened to me but because of the things that have happened to me. I know that without a shadow of a doubt that God has been with me from the beginning and the reason why I know it is because I am still alive and able to do for myself.

As we work to press towards the mark, we must all remember that whatever pace that you are moving in is okay and to stay focused on your path and not look to the left or right at anyone else's because our walk is just that, ours. No one has the right to tell you that your pace is not right. We are all different and entitled to our differences. This life that we are so graciously given should at all times be cherished because at a blink of an eye it could be over. Not one moment on this earth should be taken for granted. We must take the time to really smell the roses literally.

We live in an era where everything is so rushed and fast paced never taking in the things around us. Never noticing that the sky really is blue and that grass is many different shades of green. I used to be this way and one day I was forced to take notice of the simplicities that life had to offer. When you are forced to slow down, it is the ultimate reality check. We want so much that we fail to be thankful for what we already have. This society operates in the microwave age, and no one wants to wait for anything.

It's all about getting it right now. Quick, fast, and in a hurry is the status quo for everything. Very few have perseverance. It takes dedication to endure to the end, and that is a bit difficult. Endurance is a must when you are in the Kingdom of God. As the Bible says, **"the race is not given to the swift but to those who endure to the end."**

We must all be mindful of who we are, what we are doing, and who we are doing it to. Know that in all that you do it's not done on your own accord and that you do serve a master whether you are aware of that fact or not.

Please take into account that whatever you do in this lifetime has the ability to come back to you whether that be good or bad. So I say to you, sow good seeds and learn to operate in love no matter what the next person does and know that God is always on your side no matter what it looks like.

Be mindful of the words that you put into the universe as well because there are those that are listening whether they be humans or spirits. Yes, I know that this may sound far-fetched and difficult, but I have learned from experience to expect the unexpected and that anything is possible. Take care of yourself and know that you are loved even if you don't feel it. Take time and feel the heart in your chest beating. Thump, thump, thump, thump. See, you are still alive and here on this earth for a reason. I know you may not know what that reason is, but I know, because you, yes you, are here on this earth to glorify and edify God with whatever gifts and talents He has so graciously given to you.

Now get up and go out and start living in the capacity in which God says you are to live. Embrace the freedoms that God has allowed you to have and open your heart in order to give and receive the love that is raining from my one true love, El Shaddai.

« 30 » THE SPIRITUAL IMPORTANCE OF SEX

THERE HAD BEEN TIMES in my life when I truly didn't overstand why I craved and wanted the things that I did until my relationship with God became the forefront of my life. I knew that from an early age that the human touch was very important. I also learned that it is a lie when people say that you can't miss what you have never had because the fact of the matter is, that longing for something is a sign that it is something that you have had, whether that is in the natural or the spiritual. The power of the human touch can soothe even the most savage of beasts, especially when the touch is that of the anointed.

When you have as a child been denied the basic rights of any human being it leaves a gaping hole in your life. A longing, wanting, craving, a desire, for that which the spirit knows in vital to your very survival.

The human touch is of great importance to the

healthy development of all human beings and when that basic touch is denied there is a lacking, that the spirit must have filled. For the spirit knows that the body must have certain things in order for it to function properly. The spirit that dwells within us knows us, and it knew us long before we became a human being. Therefore, the spirit will do what is require to get the physical body what it needs, when it needs it.

Now there are two sides to this equation because just as the Holy Spirit knows what we need, so does the demonic spirit. This is where the power of discernment must come into play. See, when your walk with God becomes the forefront of your life, you learn the difference between good and evil and God's voice and satan's voice. You learn that not all men are saved by God and that you have been assigned both Heavenly and hell's angels. You learn that both sets of angels are working on your behalf. God's angels want to help you succeed at the task that He has set before you and Satan's angels want to assist you in failing at the task that God has set before you.

When you are yoked with the wrong person, it causes a spiritual delay in your life. Yes, it throws your God given assignment off course. See the bible says **"be not unequally yoked with non-believers."** It also says **"where two or three are gathered together in my name, except touch and they agree, I shall be in the midst of them."** Yes, you get where I am going with this because I have spoken of this in earlier chapters. There is power in unity and in order to be touched you have to be in the presence of another.

However, in order to be touched by the right spirit, which is the spirit of Holiness, you have to be in relationship with God and know when you are in the presence of another person of God.

When this man and woman of God touch one another, there is a positive energy that is then passed through them. It is a force; The Force of God. Sex is never just sex, it is never just the physical act, it is never just for procreation. Sex when done in Holiness is a life force and healing of the body. Sex is a joining of two spirits that become one and when the oneness happens spiritual warfare begins. Those spirits began to heal those two bodies and then they are in a better position to allow the spiritual realm to use them in the way that is required for the saving of souls to take place.

The Bible says that **"the two shall join and thus become one."** Yes, one. Two spiritual beings operating on one accord. Working for the betterment of this planet and the people that inhabit it.

Sex is the man-made terminology for the act that takes place. However, the Bible calls it knowing or knew. When a man knows you, he has entered your precious gates, the holiness of you, your heaven as you will. I often preach this analogy to others as a simple form of explanation as to get you to see how this works.

The man is the plug, you know like on the end of a cord of an appliance. The woman is the outlet, you know like on the wall. God is the electricity, the current, the energy, the Power. Now let me backtrack for a moment. The Bible says that **"when a man findeth a wife he findeth a good thing and obtains favor from the Lord."**

In order for a man to be put in a position to obtain favor from God, he must first be in relationship with God. Then when in relationship with God this man will then be sent a woman of God. This woman of God then becomes a link if you will to The Most High, which opens a portal if you will to God, which in turn causes favor to rain in this man of God's life. The woman of God is the link to God's favor.

When that man of God enters that woman of God, he obtains favor from the Lord. He plugs into the outlet which in turn is the opening to the Power supply. The Source and upon plugging into the source he is then better connected to the favor of God and thus is healed, repaired, and fully anointed to go out and conquer that task which was set for him to achieve in the name of The Most High YHWH.

A man of God needs a woman of God to survive; he needs her in order to plug into the source of his power. YHWH is the source, and a man of God can only obtain that favor through that woman of God.

A plug is still a plug regardless; an outlet is still an outlet regardless. However, the plug is of no use if it doesn't have the proper outlet and the outlet is of no use if it is not connected to the proper power supply. That woman must be a woman of God in relationship with the Source in order for this to work for both of them because that man can plug into that woman all day long and still not obtain favor. The condition must be right. Yes, procreation can still happen, but the true oneness and the favor will not be there. There will still be an emptiness, a gaping hole if you will.

That is why we have so many unfaithful people roaming this planet because they are searching for that which they know that they need in order to obtain the Lords favor and they don't even realize that in order to obtain that favor they must first be in relationship with God. True relationship requires sacrifice and real examination of ones-self with an overstanding of whose you are and why you are on this planet.

You must also know that imposters will be sent your way and that you will sometimes even as an anointed child of God be tricked into thinking that they are the one because Satan is clever. That's why as soon as you realize that you have been led astray you must end it right away and do what is required to get back on course to your favor.

No, this will not be an easy task because if it were everyone would be successful at it. However, you can't give up just because the road is a little bumpy. I know because for me it has come from a place of experience. It has not been easy, and it still isn't easy. Being real never is easy when we live in a society where being fake is the new real. I refuse to pretend any longer. I embrace every facet of who and whose I am. That includes acknowledging that I need to be plugged into by my Divine Partner on a regular basis just as I need food to nourish my body, I need him to nourish my spirit. I am a human being that is inhabited by a spiritual being. I am first a spiritual being and then I am a human being. I am continuously connected to my Source and filled with the Power of YHWH.

"I AM that which I AM" because I am created in His image and likeness. I bask in that fact now, and I relish at the thought that I am created from THE SOURCE. I am THE SOURCE because HE says that I am.

The spiritual and the physical aspects of sex do have some similarities as well as some differences. Therefore, we can't explore one without exploring the other. The physical side of sex or the knowing of a person comes with great benefits to the natural body, and also, it comes with great and deadly consequences if you indulge in the activities with the wrong person.

Let's now explore the benefits of a healthy and active sex life with your Divine partner. Is Sex Really That Important? Yes, it actually is. As more and more research is done on the subject, it's becoming clearer that having healthy sex is essential to a healthy life—and that sex can even help you to live longer.

Sex Fights Colds and the Flu, so people who have sex a couple of times a week tend to have significantly higher amounts of the antibody immunoglobulin A (IgA) than those who have sex

less than once a week. What does that mean? "IgA is the first line of defense against colds and flu."

Sex Burns Calories because sex increases blood flow, and gets your heart pumping. Simply put, sex is a form of exercise, and it's more fun than running laps.

Sex Reduces Risk of Heart Disease and numerous studies have shown that an active sex life is closely correlated with longer life. Specifically, it seems like sex may lower the risk for heart attacks, strokes, and other heart diseases.

Sex Regulates Hormone Levels. Why should you care? Well, among other things, a healthy hormone profile promotes regular menstrual cycles and decreases negative menopause symptoms.

Sex Cures Headaches and Reduces Physical Pain. Although it doesn't seem like sex would help relieve a headache, it actually does. How? During sex, the hormone oxytocin is released in your body, and oxytocin reduces pain.

Sex Reduces Stress and Lowers Blood Pressure. Another benefit of the oxytocin released during orgasm: it calms the nerves. Sex also helps you sleep better. When he rolls over and starts snoring after a good bout in the bed, it's not just physical exhaustion. Oxytocin not only calms you down but it also specifically promotes sleep.

Sex Reduces Risk for Prostate Cancer. "The claim

physiologically," by researcher "is that if you empty out the tank every so often, it's healthier than holding onto the material within the tank."

Sex Reduces Risk for Breast Cancer. Women can get in on this sex-as-preventive-care thing too. According to researchers, studies show that "women who have vaginal intercourse often have less risk of breast cancer than those who do not.

Sex Boosts Self-Esteem and Improves Mood. The psychological benefits of a healthy sex life are many. The feeling of walking around on cloud nine after sex lasts longer than you think. According to researchers, a healthy sex life leads to long-term satisfaction with one's mental health and enhances your ability to communicate honestly and intimately. People who are sexually active are less likely to have alexithymia, which is a personality trait characterized by the inability to express or understand emotions.

In other words, people having sex can express themselves better.

Sex Prevents Preeclampsia. Preeclampsia is a fairly common condition in which hypertension arises during pregnancy. Interestingly enough, a number of studies have shown that if a woman has had enough exposure to her partner's semen prior to conception, she is significantly less likely to get preeclampsia. In fact, tests conducted by Dutch biologists in 2000 confirmed that there is an especially significant reduced risk of preeclampsia for women who regularly practice oral sex—and even more of a reduced risk for those who swallow their partner's semen.

Sex Improves Sense of Smell. Scientists knew for a long time that the hormone prolactin surges in both men and women after orgasm. Then, in 2003, a team of Canadian researchers discovered that, in mice, prolactin causes stem cells in the brain to develop new neurons in the brain's olfactory bulb—its smell center. One of the researchers, said that he suspects that the increase in prolactin levels after sex helps "forge memories that are part of mating behaviors."

Sex Increases Bladder Control. The pelvic thrusting involved in sex exercises the Kegel muscles. These are the same set of muscles that controls urine flow. So lots of sex now may help prevent the onset of incontinence later.

Now isn't this all amazing information. See, some of you have been really missing out on the healthy benefits by denying yourself sexually intercourse because of whatever reasons. Please look at the deeper meaning of sex and its benefits to the human mind, body, and spirit.

In order for the spirits to totally connect after the bodies join in the sexual act, you must slow down. The slowing down allows you to not only totally connect on all three levels, but it also allows you to feel all of the emotions within the act itself and to feel the energy within the beings.

When you are in a hurry to complete the deed you miss out on the joining of the spirits and the true meaning of having sex with the one you are designed to be with. That's why we have such a major disconnect between man and woman and one of the reasons for the cheating and infidelity.

When you rush your bodies during the sexual act you receive that burst of adrenaline but as soon as the act is over, you feel empty, dirty, shame, and guilt. There is no staying power, no longevity. A couple of the reasons behind these feelings are because you were with the wrong person and you did not have a spiritual connection with that being and by spiritual I mean Holy and Divine, for there is a great difference between having sex with a God sent being and a demonic sent being.

When we step out of the will of God, we do open ourselves up to further demonic attack and possible engulfment. So please, be aware who you share your Divine Spirit with, for even the bible speaks of, **"demon inhabitants having sex with human beings."**

Sex is a beautiful thing in its totality when done the right way and for the right reasons and of course with the right person. If you do not have a healthy sex life, you need to examine the reasons why and come up with a solution to fix it because it is of great benefit to you in doing so.

Yes, I know that some would have you think that sex

is not important and that it is even meaningless but please don't be fooled into thinking that rubbish because sex is a very vital part of us being spiritual as well as us being human and sex was created for more than just procreation. The intimate act of sex can be the gateway to Heaven when it is used in its proper form.

Which brings me to the downside of sex as with all things there is both good and bad. I pray that when this chapter is complete that you will have a greater over-standing of why you should be responsible and safe when indulging in the act of knowing another individual on what I know to be a sacred and biblical act of the Divine Spirit and the body joining in a transference of energies.

When you engage in a sexual act with a person that you are not equally joked with nor divinely linked with, you create a negative energy base. So instead of you becoming energized, you end up drained and feeling low, dirty, ashamed, and sad after the act. That is your Divine Spirit telling you that you have invaded a sacred and Holy place with evil and demonics. That the very positive act that was supposed to bring about a greater awakening in the two parties involved has now become a negative act bringing about discord, hurt, and feelings of loss.

Yes, during the act, it feels good, and you feel alive and purposeful even, but you soon realize that it was all a trick. That you in fact just gave away a chunk of your soul.

With a knowing of someone also comes a responsibility that most aren't even aware of and those that are, do not want the responsibility. The act of sex should always be a loving one. A one of both giving and thus receiving.

Sex takes a turn for the worse when you start to practice and crave certain things. When you engage in what is deemed to be demonic sexual acts, you open yourself up to the horrors that come along with it. For instance, having sex with animals is beastly but many people practice this on a daily basis and find nothing wrong with it. To engage in a sacred act with an animal is nothing short of evil. You are having intercourse outside that which is your life form. So what do you expect to happen in the spirit realm when you do these things. Some would call this taboo but this goes far beyond being taboo, it is demonic.

When you open yourself to these kinds of acts, you open yourself up to other forms of brutal and sadistic acts as well. It becomes a craving for that which is not natural. You have opened up a portal to the demonic world when you engage in these beastly acts.

An act of sexual intercourse is also a transferring of physical and spiritual DNA and negative and positive energy, and this is not just from a human standpoint. So you had better realize that this is far deeper than you know. When you engage in certain acts, you are opening yourself up to a greater demonic engulfment.

Sex can be a very beautiful thing when done right but on the flip side of that sex can be a very ugly thing as well. When we think about child rape, adult rape, sexual torture, intercourse with animals, forced sodomy, sexual release by murder, and etc., you must by now know that there is power in sex, and that power can be both negative and positive.

There is a powerful energy that is released when you engage in sex. That energy has a life force behind it, and that life force should always be YHWH but as with all things, there is both good and bad. There is a world of spiritual demons awaiting to inhabit a body so that they can perform such acts. These negative forces know that if they can get you to do certain things that it gives them a greater power over you and one of the greatest of these negative powers are the STD'S that you are left to deal with. The Spiritually Transmitted Demons!

So far we have just spoken on the spiritual aspects of the sex gone wrong thing. Oh but dear Lord, there is a natural side to sex gone wrong as well, and it is called STD's, yes sexually transmitted diseases. There it is, the dark side of having sex with the wrong person, it can bring about diseases and mind you some of these diseases have no cure, and others are DEADLY! I suggest you go to **www.cdc.gov** and read the very long list of sexually transmitted diseases and the symptoms.

There are a lot of risks that come with having sex and the more you have unprotected sex with the wrong person the greater the risk. As I have stated before sex can be a very beautiful thing when done right and with the right person. We can only learn as we go and know that each one of us carry the responsibility for ourselves and the ones that we chose to have sex with.

Our choices and those of others are to be made based on the truth. You have no right to deceive someone in order to get what you want from them. They have a right to know the truth and to base their decision to be with you on the whole truth, not some made up fabrication that you present to them.

There is a spiritual responsibility as well to having sex with someone because it is not just the joining of flesh that is involved. It is also the joining of spirits. **"The two shall thus join and become one,"** so be forewarned that not all spirits are of the Holy; there are those that are also demonic.

Demonic attachment is a very real danger when having sex with the wrong person. YHWH created one man for one woman and no matter how many people you have sex with, you were only created to be with one and only one being.

When you aren't with your Divine Partner your soul searches and seeks this person. That is why you have a yearning and an emptiness after you have sex with the wrong person. The Spirit wants its Divine Partner, and until you are united with that person, you will forever be yearning.

Most would like to think that this is a sign that you aren't ready for commitment, but it is really a sign that you aren't with the right one. Cheating is an announcement that you aren't where you need to be. It is a sign that that which is need has not yet been found. It is a painful truth that most don't want to face, and it is a lie that we are not faithful by nature or shall I use the politically correct term not monogamous.

That is a coward's way of saying I won't take responsibility for my actions so I will use what society lies and says about nature to keep doing what I want without repercussions.

« APPENDIX »

THANKFUL

I AM THANKFUL FOR the journey that this life has taken me on. My life and all that I hope to be is because of who I am in the sight of El Shaddai. The emptiness that I have felt my entire life in this human body has only been filled by the Holy Spirit. I embrace and accept who I am in the body of The Almighty. As painful as this life has been for me, I will not give up, let up, nor hold up, for this is my destiny. I am predestined to be who I am and there is no changing that.

I am walking in my purpose. I am not becoming who I thought I needed to be. I am however finally functioning and operating as who I have always been. I am so thankful to God for pushing me to accept who I am and for teaching me how to allow that which needs to be, to be. I am not longer afraid of my spiritual gifts. I am finally at a place in my life where I am actually embracing my gifts and welcoming them. I now look forward to what my spirit is going to show me next and I no longer have the longing to be that which I know that I already am.

I am encouraged when I see the woman I am. I can even smile at the thought of all I have had to endure in order to allow her to burst forward and take the reins. I am excited to know that I am no longer pretending to be someone that I am not. I am living in my reality and I am proud of that fact. See, it is that spiritual reality that has me smiling at myself because that gives me hope that all that I have endured was not in vain. It was because I was continuously denying who YHWH knew that I was and needed me to be. All of the suffering was due to this fact. I want all YHWH wants for me and I want my spirit to continue to lead me in order for my flesh to operate in the fullness thereof. The spirit is always before the flesh. It is unfortunate that this society thinks that the body rules, it is this misconception that gets us in trouble in the spirit realm and in the natural. The denial of the spirit always leads us astray.

I am very aware that the body has needs and I am aware that the spirit has needs. I am also aware that when the spiritual needs are met first then the needs of the body will surely follow. The spirit will make sure that the body has what it needs. We must first allow the spirit to do what is required. Always know that we are first SPIRITUAL and then NATURAL. SELAH.

« NOTES »

Chapter 1
Breaking The Cycle of Abuse
Contains quotes from the KJV Bible.
Also quotes from unknown sources learned during childhood.

Chapter 2
Expecting the Unexpected
Contains quotes from the KJV Bible.
Also contains quotes from the Obama 2008 Presidential Campaign.

Chapter 3
Seasons
Contains quotes from the KJV Bible.
Also contains quotes from Japanese Poetry Haiku.

Chapter 4
Learning to Live Again
Contains quotes from the KJV Bible.
Also contains quotes from Webster's Dictionary.

Chapter 5
Distance
Contains quotes from the KJV Bible.
Also contains quotes from the movie, What's Love Got to Do with It.

Chapter 6
Contradictions
Contains quotes from the KJV Bible.

Chapter 7
Is It Really
Contains quotes from the KJV Bible.
Also contains quotes from Webster's Dictionary.

Chapter 8
People Pleaser
Contains quotes from the KJV Bible.

Chapter 9
To Thine Own-Self Be True
Contains quotes from the KJV Bible.

Chapter 10
Reflection
Contains quotes from the KJV Bible.
Also contains quotes from unknown sources learned in childhood.

Chapter 11
Wanting
Contains quotes from the KJV Bible.
Also contains quotes from William Shakespeare.

Chapter 12
Honoring The Power of Two
Contains quotes from the KJV Bible.

Chapter 13
Expectation is Manifestation
Contains quotes from the KJV Bible.

Chapter 14
Christ Not Karma
Contains quotes from the KJV Bible.

Chapter 15
Selfless
Contains quotes from the KJV Bible.

Chapter 16
Spirit Verses Natural
Contains quotes from the KJV Bible.

Chapter 17
The Power of Suggestion
Contains quotes from the KJV Bible.

Chapter 18
A Virtuous Woman
Contains quotes from the KJV Bible.

Chapter 19
Attracting a True Man of God
Contains quotes from the KJV Bible.

Chapter 20
Who Holds the Key
Contains quotes from the KJV Bible.

Chapter 21
Hurry Up and Wait
Contains quotes from the KJV Bible.

Chapter 22
Acknowledge
Contains quotes from the KJV Bible.

Chapter 23
Decisions
Contains quotes from the KJV Bible.
Also contains quotes from Webster's Dictionary, Jim Crow, and unknown source learned from childhood.

Chapter 24
Preparations
Contains quotes from the KJV Bible.
Also contains quotes from William Shakespeare, African American Kwanzaa Celebration, African Proverbs, and Malcolm X.

Chapter 25
Moving Forward with God's Covering
Contains quotes from the KJV Bible.

Chapter 26
Backwards
Contains quotes from the KJV Bible.
Also contains quotes from Webster's Dictionary.

Chapter 27
Knowing the Female Body
Contains quotes from the KJV Bible.
Also contains quotes from the CDC and Women's Health.

Chapter 28
Africa the Motherland
Contains quotes from the KJV Bible.

Chapter 29
At Your Own Pace
Contains quotes from the KJV Bible.

Chapter 30
The Spiritual Importance of Sex
Contains quotes from the KJV Bible.
Also contain quotes from the CDC.

« LINKS »

Research and quotes were also used from online sources:

www.biblegateway.com
www.merriamwebster.com
www.yhwh.com
www.cdc.gov
www.whitehouse.gov
www.officialkwanzaawebsite.org
www.interestingafricafacts.com

« LINKS TO AUTHOR »

www.victoriaamidou.com
www.facebook.com/victoriaamidou
www.twitter.com/victoriaamidou
www.instagram.com/victoriaamidou
www.youtube.com/victoriaamidou
www.periscope.com/victoriaamidou

« OVERVIEW »

As you have noticed in many of the chapter's in El Shaddai the word overstand is used instead of understand. This is done for the simple fact that under is beneath and over is above. Therefore, an overstanding is needed in every situation for the betterment of ones, self. **Selah.**